RON RANSOM CARVES

ATHLETIC SANTA Mini-Cheers©

Text written with and photography by Jeffrey B. Snyder

Step-by-step instructions plus patterns for 5 original Santas

Schiffer Publishing Ltd
77 Lower Valley Road, Atglen, PA 19310

Dedication

To my youngest grandson, Robert, who I almost birthed on the way to the hospital at 2:00 AM in the morning and my friend Ardie Hazlequist who introduced me to the carving knife.

ISBN: 0-88740-825-7
Printed in Hong Kong

Library of Congress Cataloging-in-Publication Data

Ransom, Ron.
Ron Ransom carves athletic Santa mini-cheers: step-by-step instructions plus patterns for 5 original Santas/text written with a and photography by Jeffrey B. Snyder.
p. cm. –(a Schiffer book for woodcarvers)
ISBN 0-88740-825-7 (pbk.)
1. Wood-carving–Patterns. 2. Wood-carved figurines. 3. Santa Claus in art. I. Snyder, Jeffrey B. II. Title. III. Title: Athletic Santa mini-cheers. IV. Series.
TT199.7.R357
731.4'62--dc20 95-7003
CIP

Published by Schiffer Publishing, Ltd.
77 Lower Valley Road
Atglen, PA 19310
Please write for a free catalog.
This book may be purchased from the publisher.
Please include $2.95 postage.
Try your bookstore first.

We are interested in hearing from authors
with book ideas on related subjects.

Contents

Introduction

These are the Santas we will be carving and the tools we will use to carve them. Each of the steps illustrated here can still be done with a knife, but I've found that gouges speed up the work.

One of the most exciting times ever was the announcement that the '96 Olympics would be held in my birthplace, Atlanta, Georgia. After being a part of public recreation for thirty years, both as a planner and participant, I had an urge to do some additional sports-type Santas to commemorate the event.

I hope you enjoy trying these, as well as the quilt and tree holding Santas. All sports related Santas have been good sellers for me and the "quilt guy" is one of the first to go at the shop where I sell my carvings. I have also shown variations of the basic pattern of the Santa athletes, which should stimulate other ideas.

In the past, many of you have told me you enjoyed my miniatures (or Mini-Cheers) and were able to move a lot of your scraps, inspiring this book. Drop me a line and if you need a question answered include a self-addressed, stamped envelope.

Ron Ransom
Box 4101
Marietta, GA 30061

Tools, etc.

As with most carvers, I have tried a great number of tools, sharpening methods and styles. I find that I enjoy my method of carving best and envy those who do the difficult pieces. For want of a better excuse, I'll use "You can't teach an old dog new tricks." I think this dog is probably a little lazy.

I like the knives made by Bob Lominack. They come extremely sharp and hold an excellent edge, requiring only occasional sharpening. Bob can be reached at P.O. Box 1189, Abingdon, VA 24212.

The various gouges are from a set of Swiss made, palm handled carving sets sent to me from Woodcraft. The numbers I show in the texts of my last two books correspond to this set. Woodcraft and many others sell fine tools and equipment. I've found a MINIMITE drill from Dremel to be useful in tight areas. It will also do fine detailing.

As I have said before, if you are not a member of the National Woodcarvers Association, you should be. Their bi-monthly issues are loaded with information on what other carvers are doing, patterns and just about everything a beginning or advanced carver needs to know.

Annual membership dues are eight dollars and include a subscription to the magazine "Chip Chats." Foreign memberships are ten dollars annually. The address is:

National Woodcarver's Association
P.O. Box 43218
Cincinnati, OH 45243

Boxer Santa

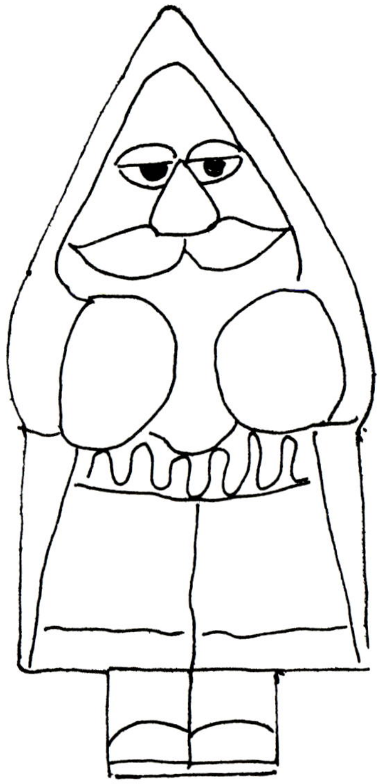

Start by rounding the edges of this Santa.

We are going into the Olympic arena now. We'll carve a boxer first. This basic pattern will produce three Santa's in this book.

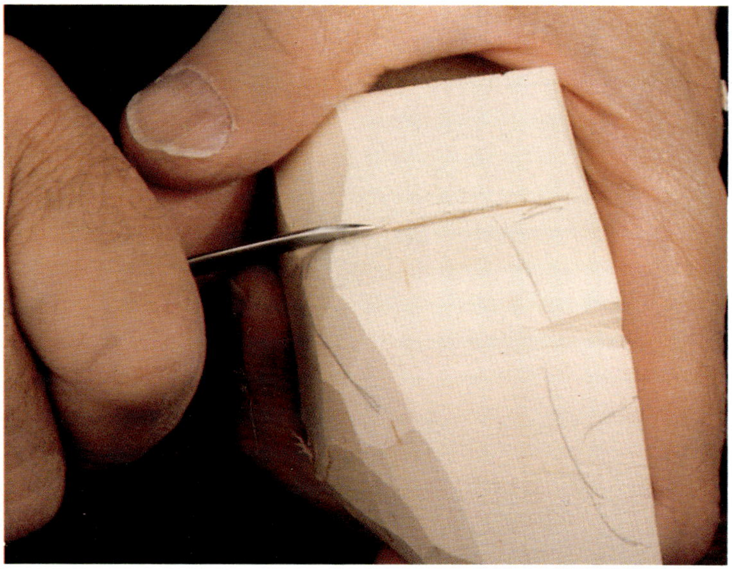

Now incise the arms.

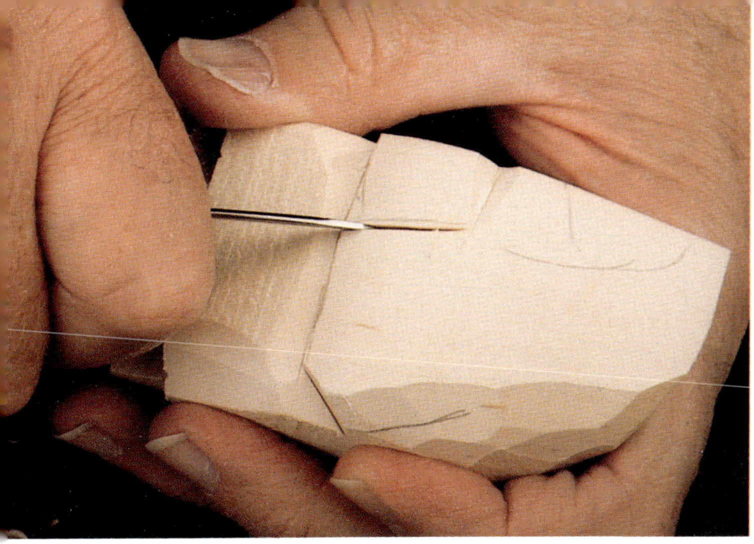

Incise the boxing glove along the pencil line.

As this is a boxing glove, you don't have to worry about the thumb, just make the glove nice and round.

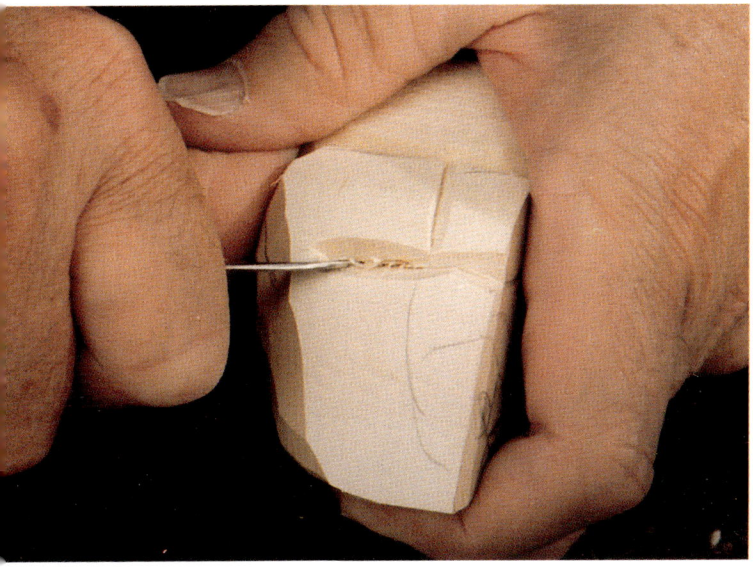

Now cut in the angle for his arms.

Cut away where the glove meets the beard in a gently angled arc.

Cut in the crook of the arm.

Incise the line of his boxing robe and reduce the wood of his trunks in front of the robe.

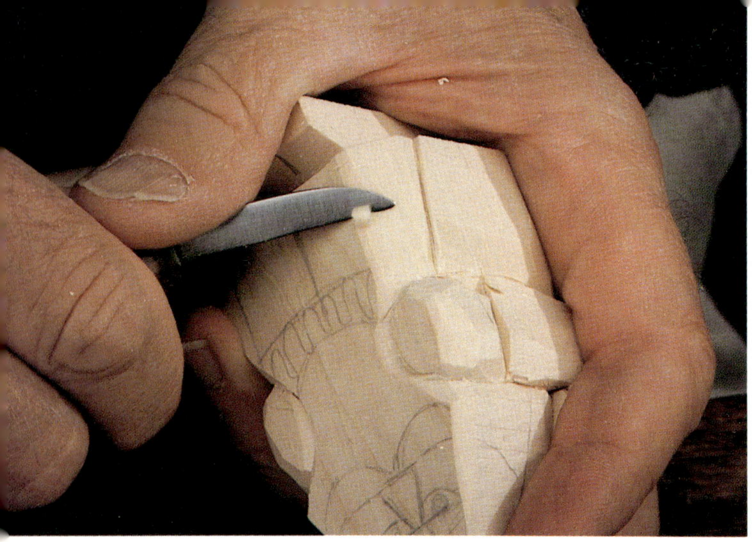

Round Santa's trunks up to his boxing gloves.

Trim out along the bottom of the waist band as well.

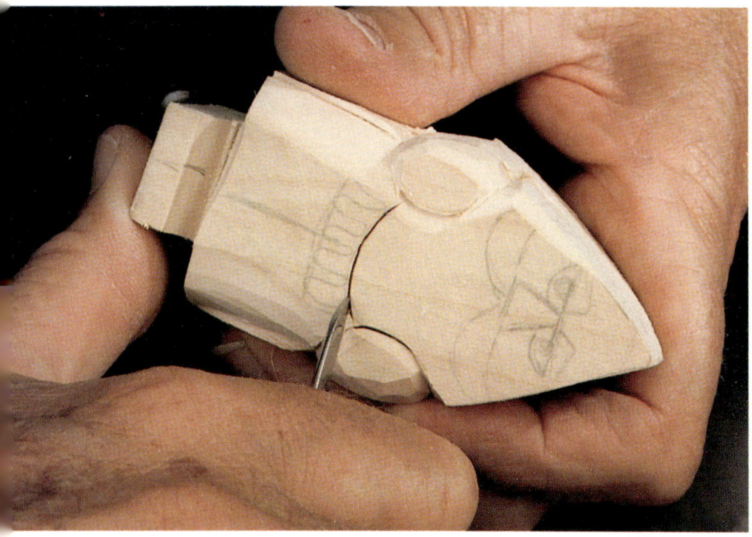

Incise the bottom of his beard where it overlaps the trunks.

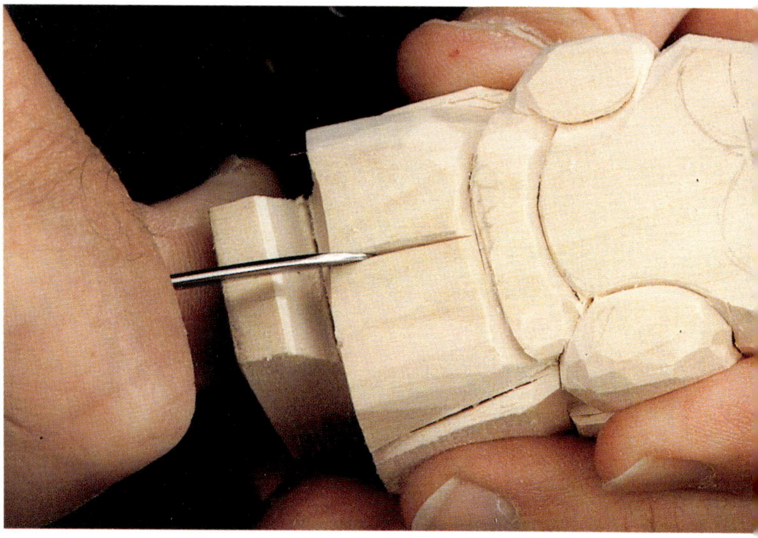

Make a nice deep line down the middle of the boxing trunks.

Trim out beneath that beard.

Come back in at an angle and take that little V out from the trunks.

We want to make these trunks fancy, so relieve above the line of the little trim at the bottom.

There is a nice sash seen on the back of the robe. Make a little incision along each line and cut back with a gentle angled cut to the incision lines.

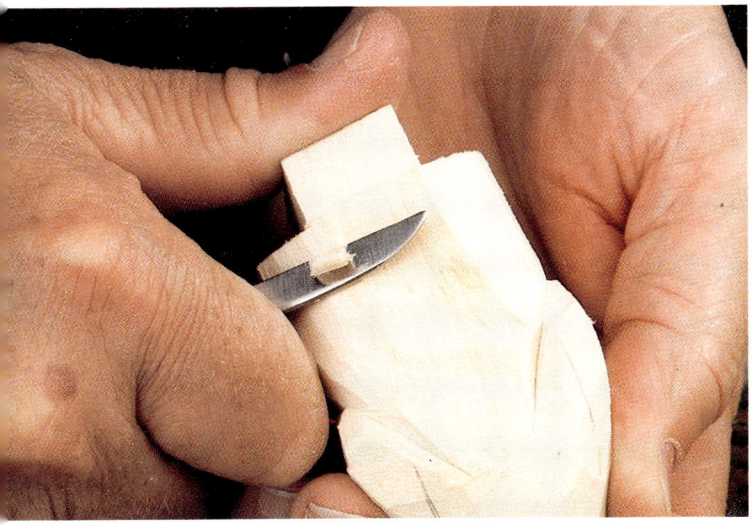

Round down the bottom of the robe now.

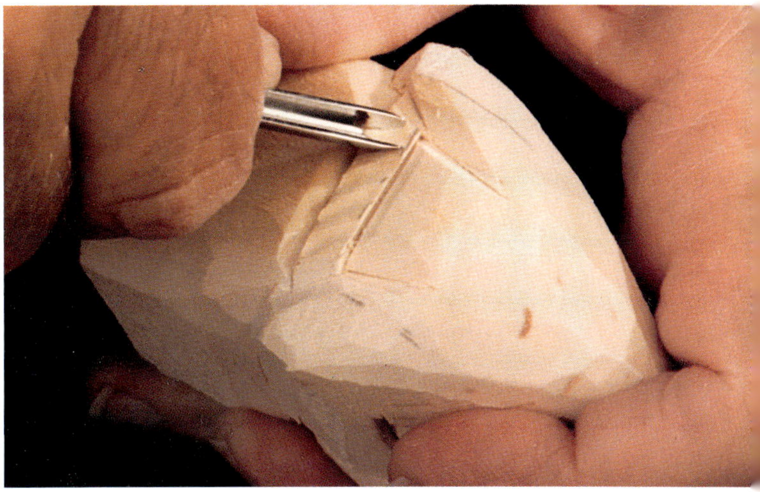

Cut the sash at an angle with the gouge to make the proper corded appearance.

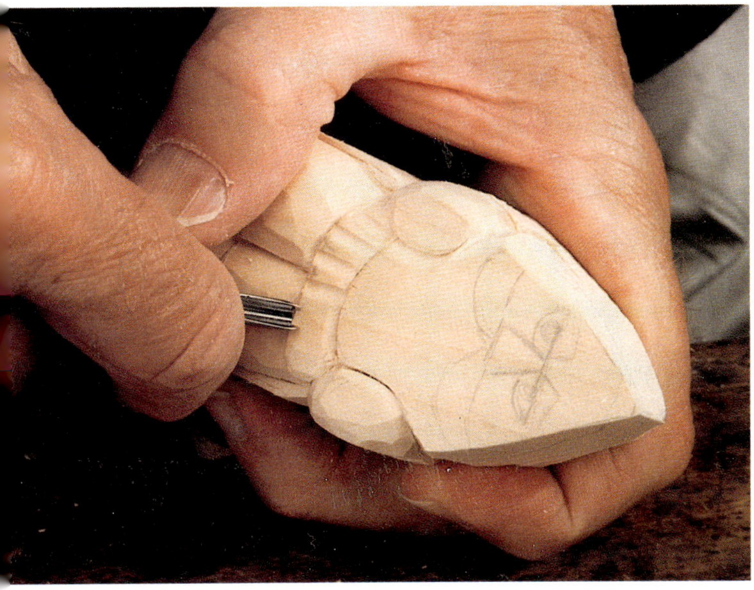

I want this band to look like elastic, so I'm using my trusty gouge to cut in evenly spaced ridges.

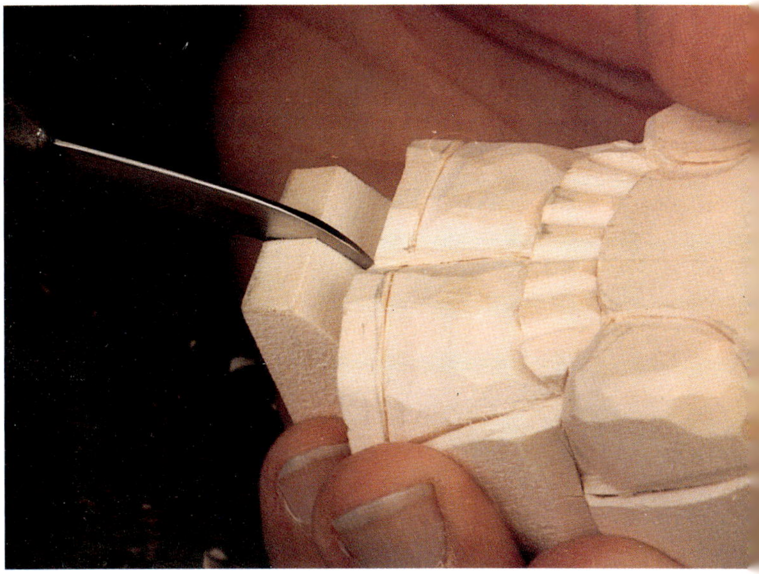

The feet are kept together, so I'm going to separate them a bit. First make a deep incision along the line.

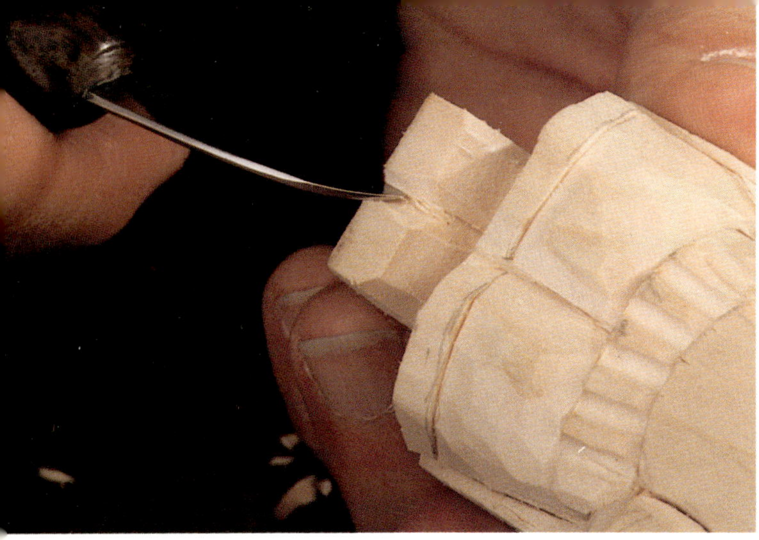

Then cut back to the incision line on either side to define each foot.

Cut in the soles with the gouge.

Repeat this process on the back of the feet.

Go back about 1/8" from the cuff to start the line for the sides of the face. Continue around to the other side.

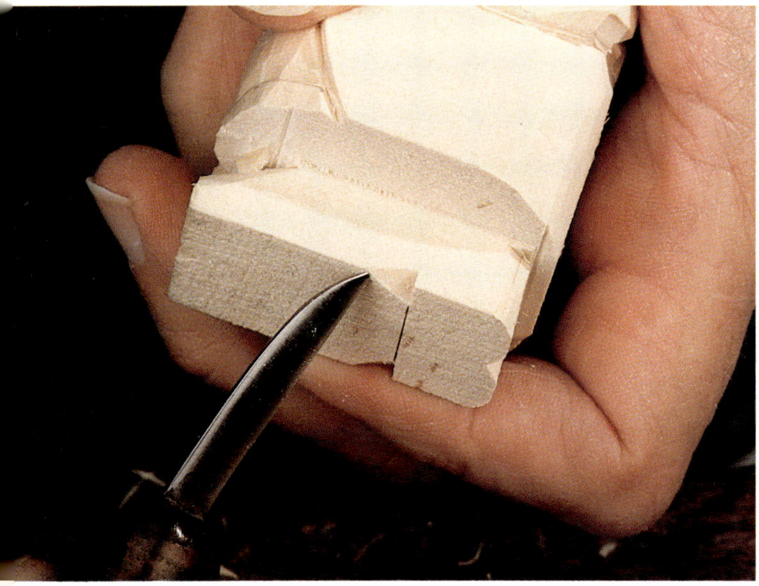

These are boxing shoes so you will have to make small notches for the heels.

Now incise along this arced line and round back to the incision line.

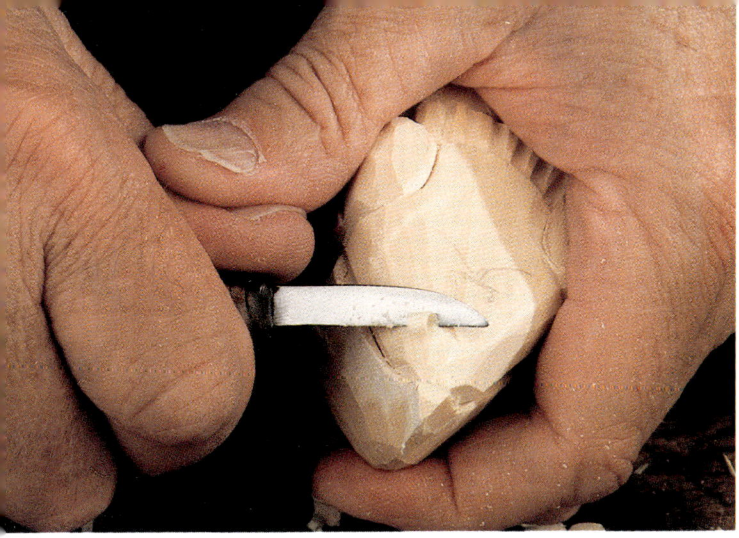

Continue rounding down the face into roughly an egg-shape. Don't worry, we'll put the lines of the face back on later.

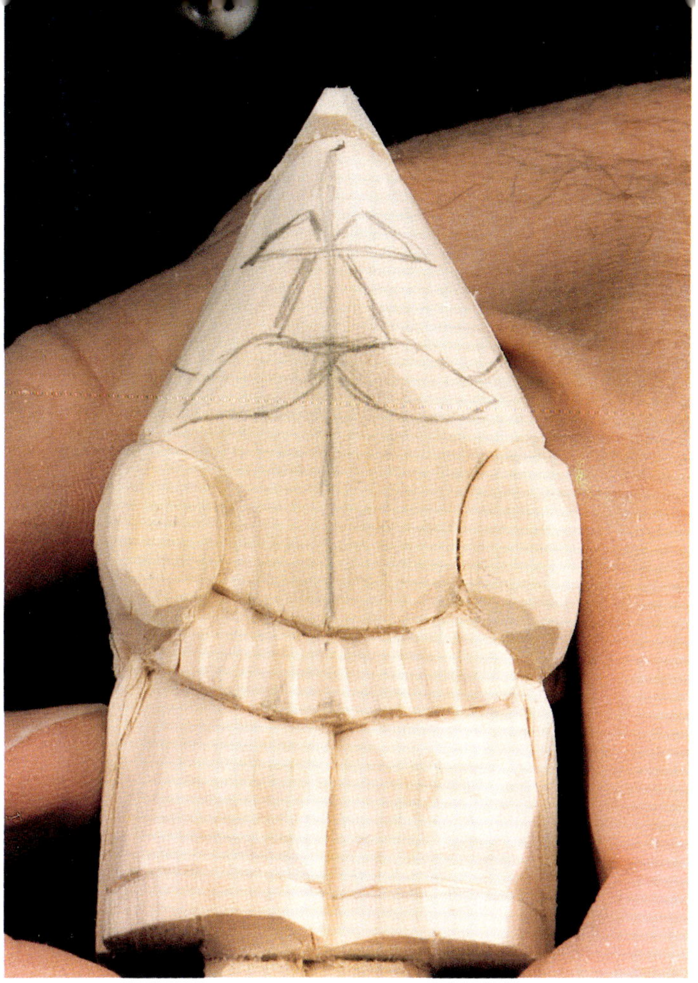

Now draw in the face again. Remember to keep the nose wide.

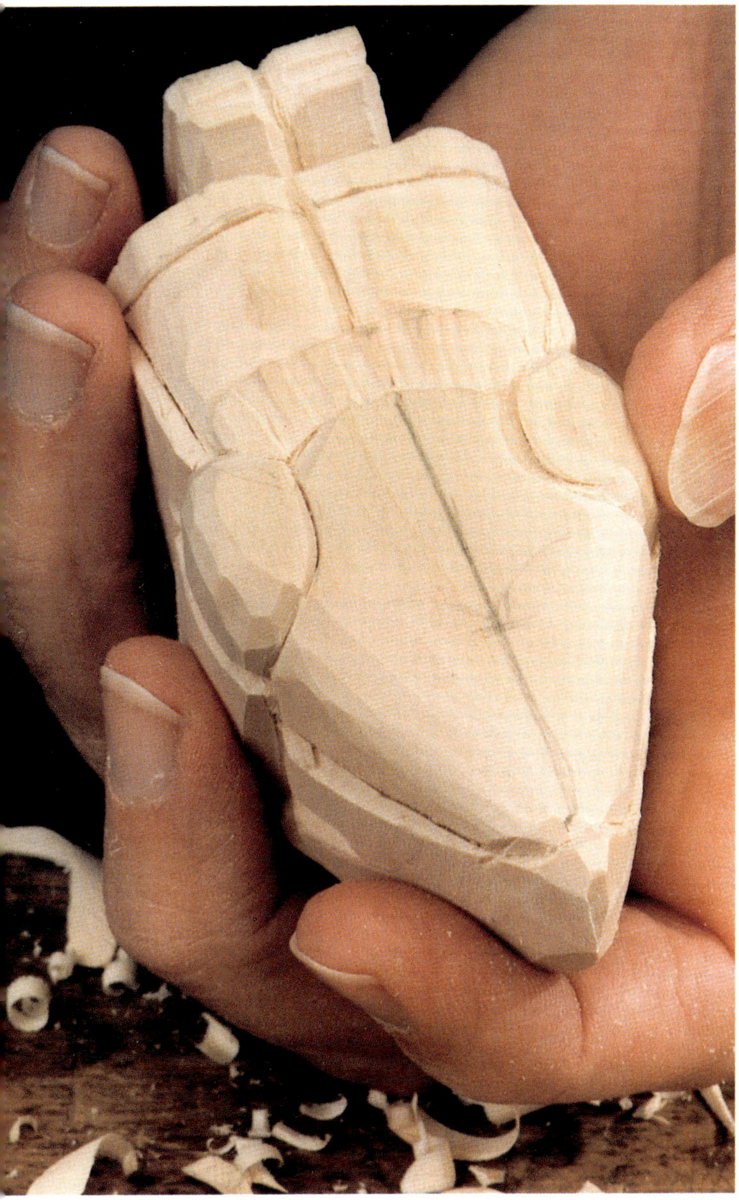

Draw in the center line of the face now.

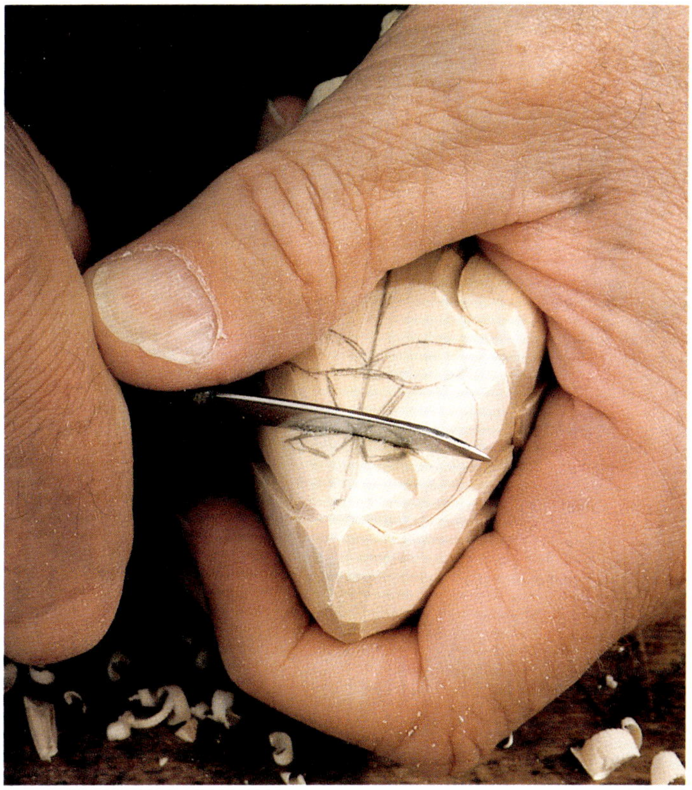

Now rock that knife into the eye channel deeply.

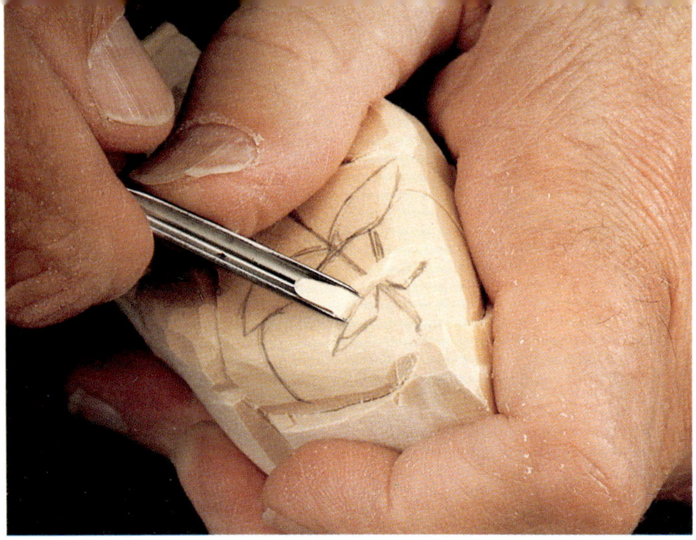

Use the gouge to cut in along the sides of the nose.

Deepen the nose a bit to give him the look of a pugilist. Not many people know that Santa boxed in college. He's thinking of coming out of retirement since George Foreman made the great comeback.

Very important: round the cheek into the mustache and beard area. This gives the Santa some good personality.

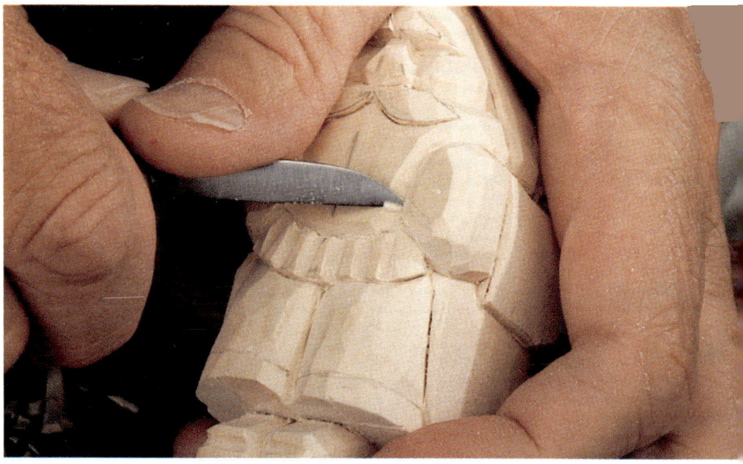

The beard is a little too flat for my liking so I'm making it a little rounder.

Incise along the line of the mustache and then trim away under the mustache along this line.

Put in some frown wrinkles around the eyes. I don't know what the difference between frown and smile wrinkles is, but as a boxer I think he should have some.

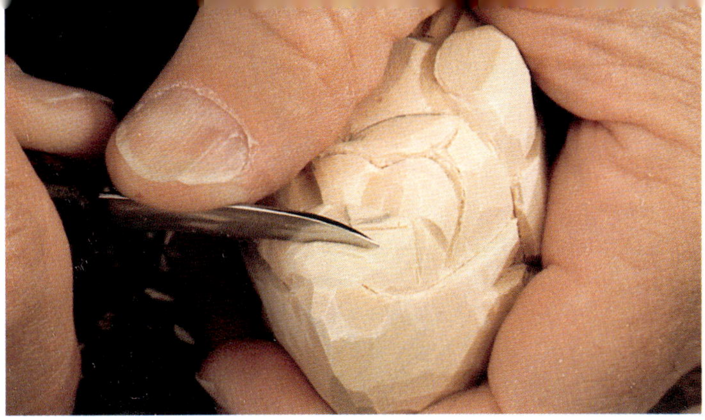

You can furrow his brow by putting your knife blade straight across the forehead and rocking it to make a very thin cut.

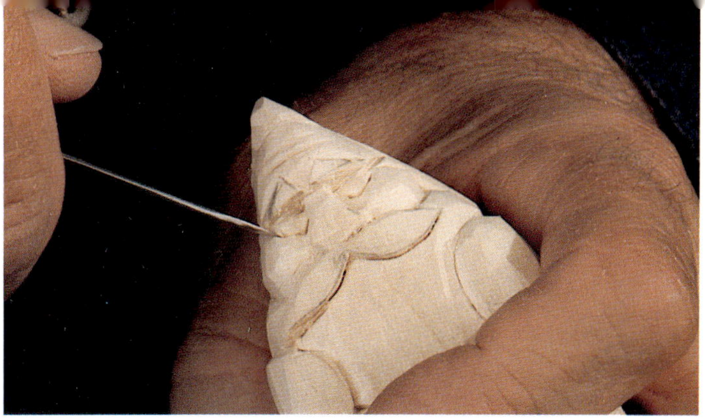

Now cut in deep along the sides of the eyes. Then make half watermelon shapes to connect with the cuts and form the eyes.

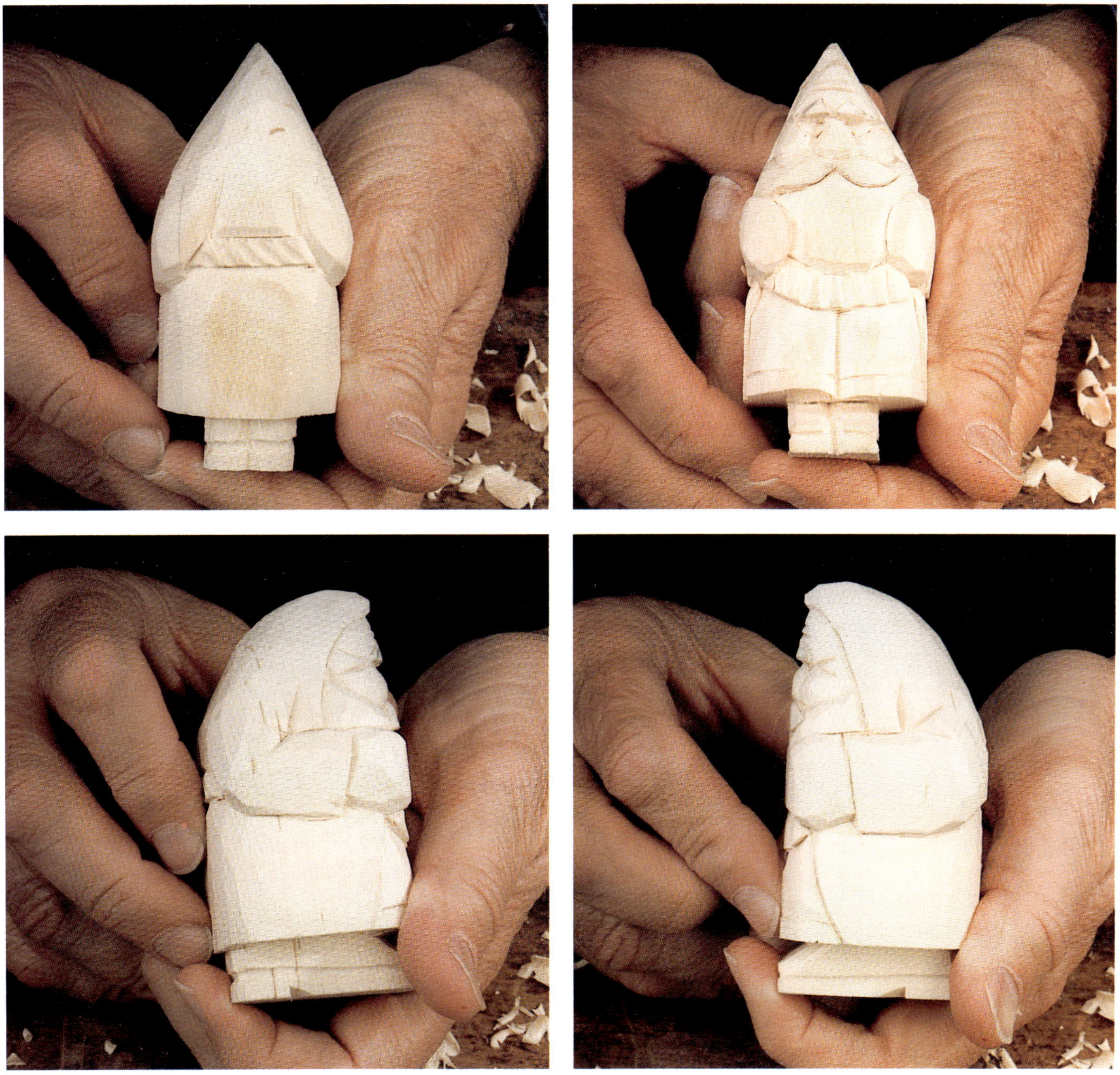

The finished carving.

Soccer Player Santa

Remove the excess wood marked in pencil here to get down to some semblance of the soccer Santa.

Transfer the pattern of the soccer Santa onto a basswood blank. These are very popular and sell well with all the new interest in the sport after the American World Cup matches.

The excess has been removed to give the rough shape to the back of the hood.

This is a healthy chunk of wood to be removed from the left arm holding the soccer ball as well. Remove the excess behind the arm. I've cut a little chunk out with the knife as a guide for the gouge. This step will help protect your hand.

Removing the excess stock with a gouge.

Start working the back so that it blends in with the arm.

Round off the back to give it some shape.

... and also where the hand and sleeve connect.

Beginning to shape the front of the left arm.

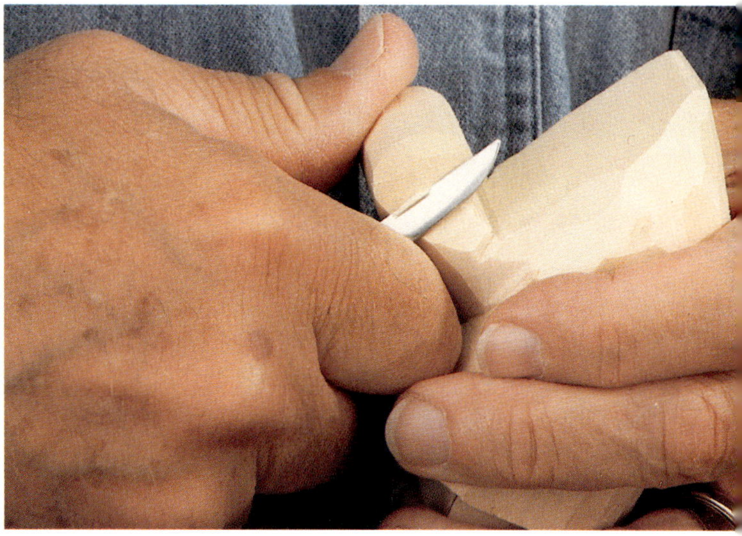

Start shaping the ball. The ball is very important to this piece. Without a good ball, this carving will fail.

Incise the front of the ball where it meets the hand ...

Draw in the hand and incise it with your knife.

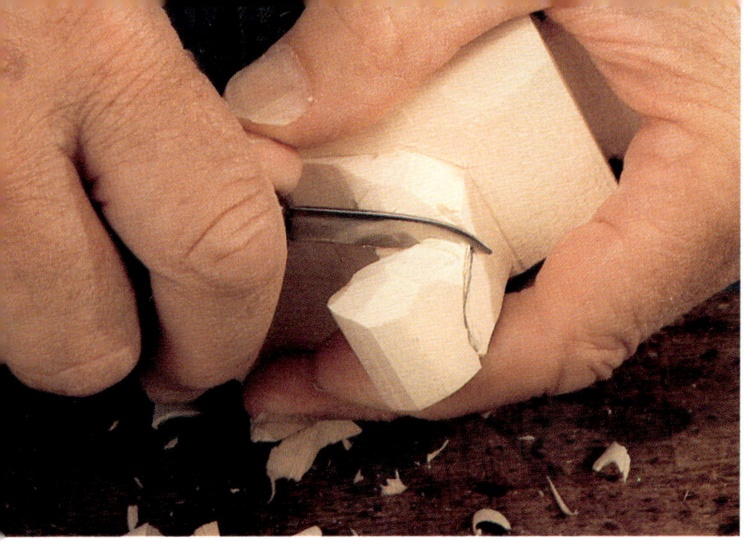

Make a little series of V cuts back and forth to get the shape of the ball where it meets the hand.

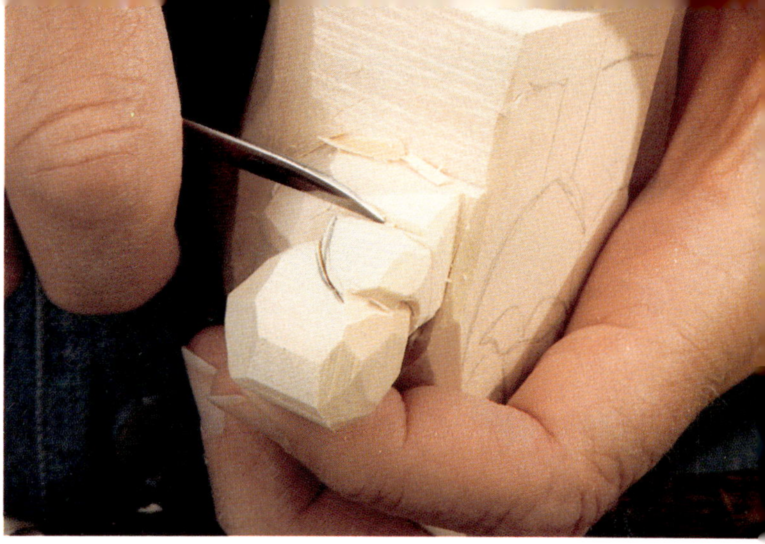

Carefully cut in where the hand and sleeve go together. Don't use much pressure or you will cut the whole hand and ball off.

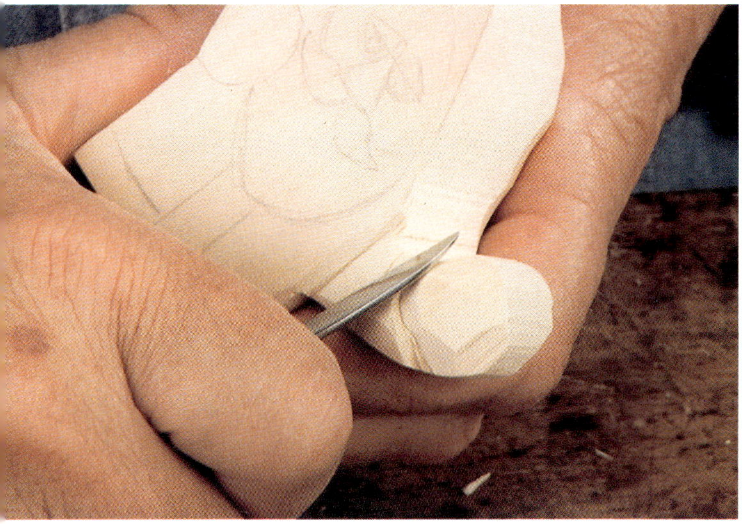

Round the ball. If you don't want to carve a ball, simply go to a craft store and buy one, carve the hand and fix the ball in place.

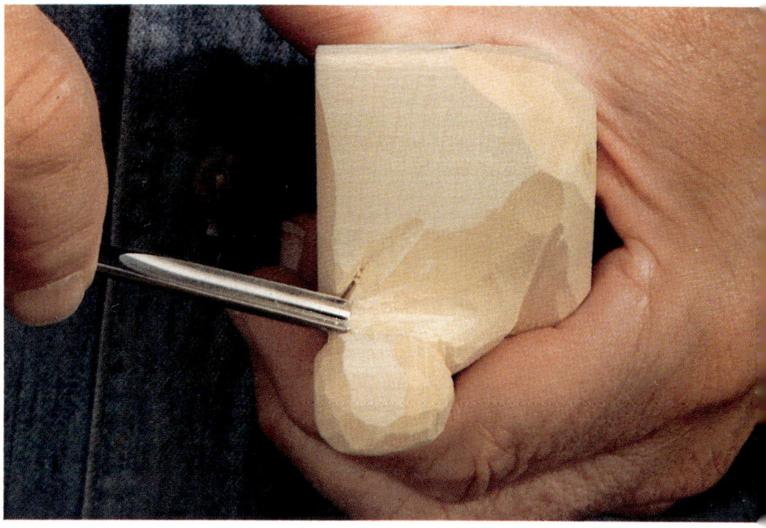

I have continued to round the ball and I am doing a little clean up on the arm with the #8 gouge.

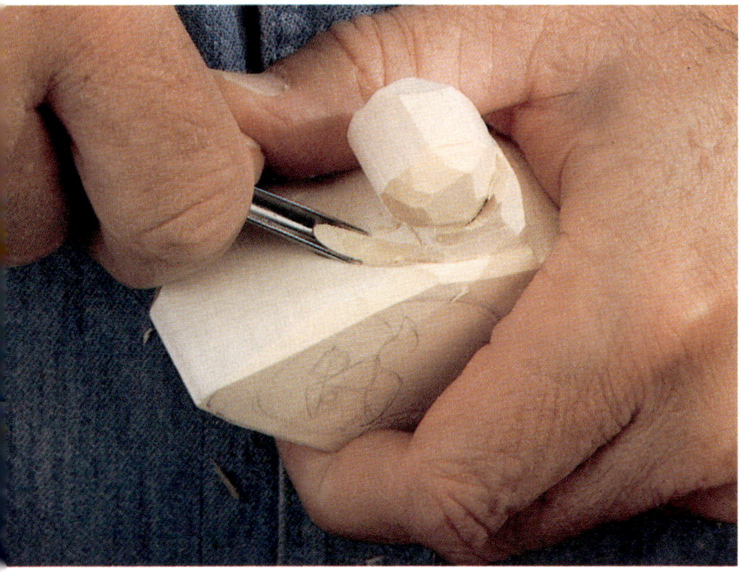

Give a little definition to the arm with a #8 gouge.

Continue to shape the arm.

Continue to round and get these edges off.

With a series of small V cuts, form the back of the right arm.

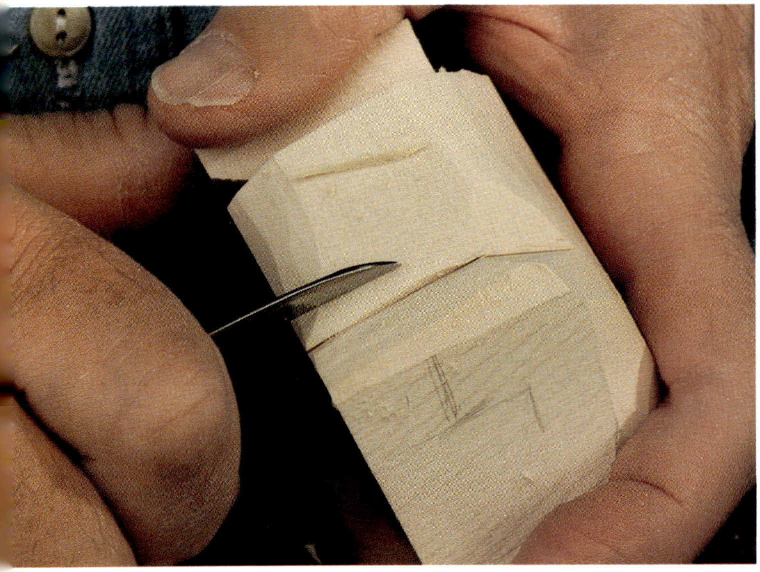

Incise the right arm and begin to round it in.

Use the #11 gouge to cut in the top part of the right arm.

The back still looks a little "humpy" so I'm going to take it down some more.

Make three little cuts with the gouge to show the folds in his sleeve.

Cut the right hand into the sleeve.

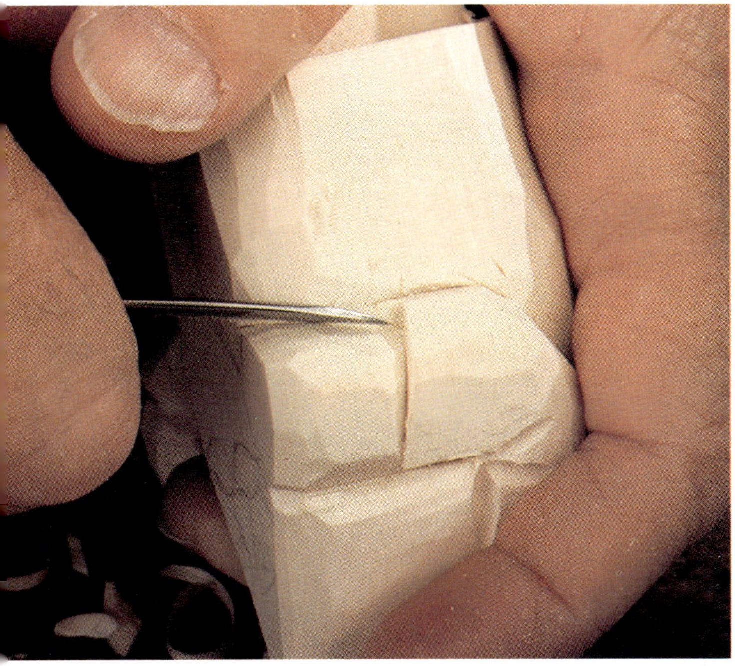

Begin to round the hand.

Incise the front of the right hand.

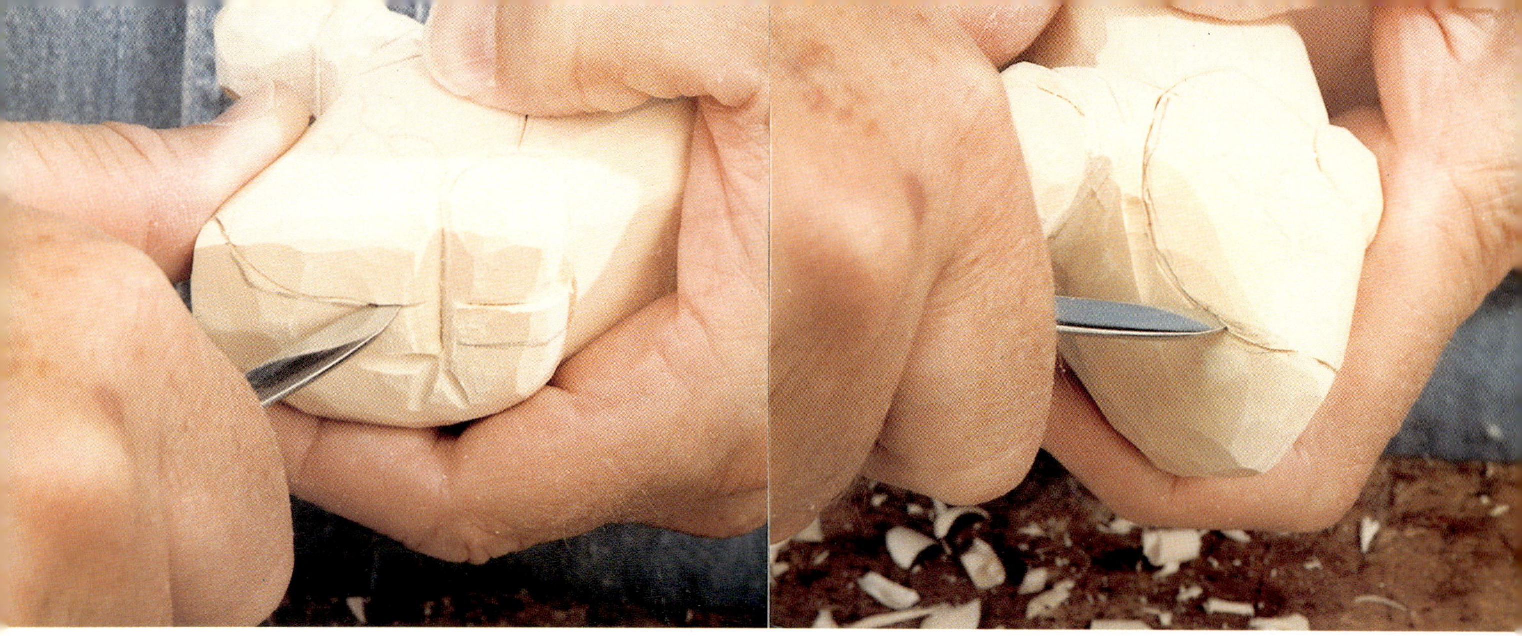

Mark in the lines where the sleeves go in and where the face should be on the side of the head. Incise the sides of the head. When you get to the left side do not rest your thumb on the hand with the ball or it will pop off.

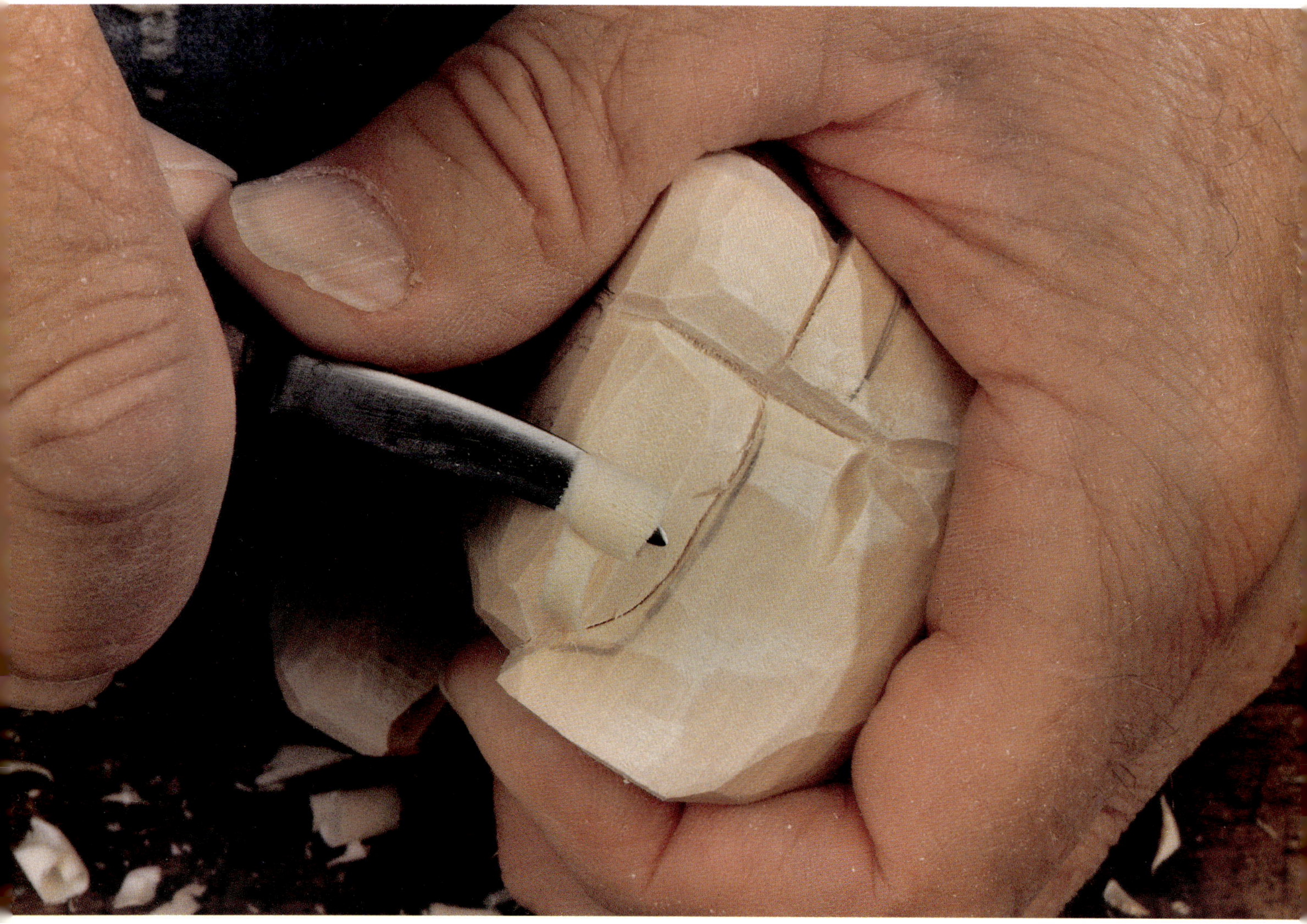

Begin to reduce the wood of the face.

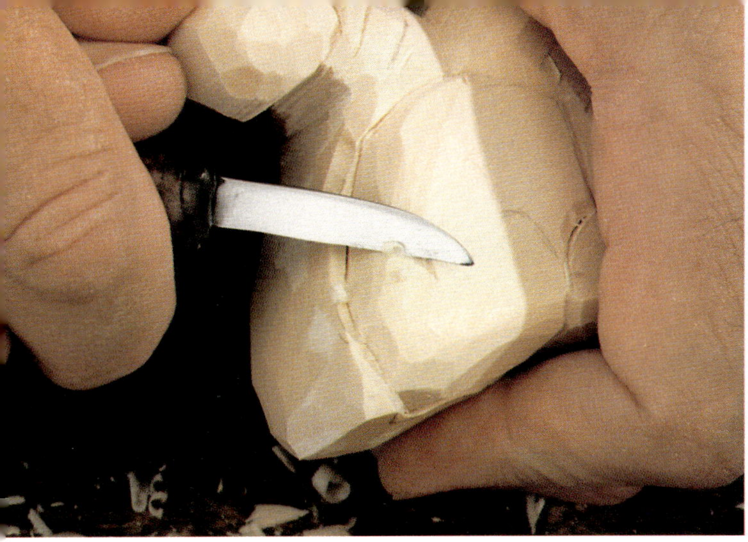

Rounding the face, using my old egg-shaped face trick.

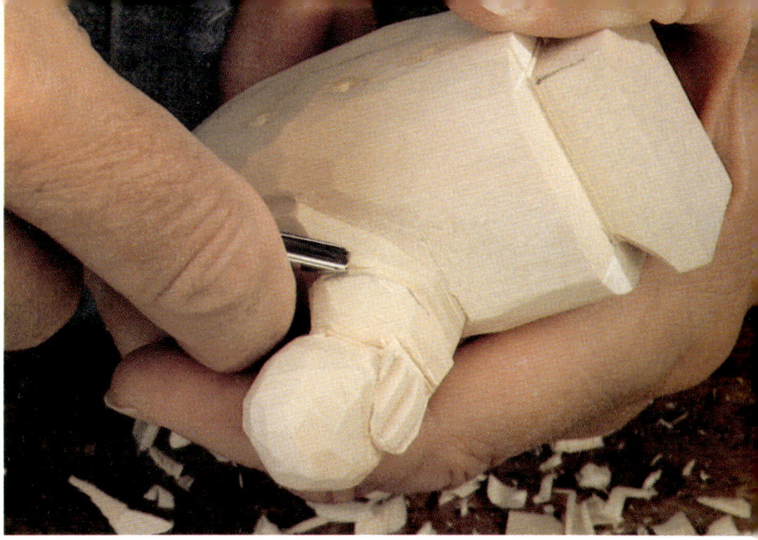

With the position of this left arm, I've found it is easier to put in the fur cuff with the #11 gouge. Let me stress again, that left arm will pop off easily if you aren't careful.

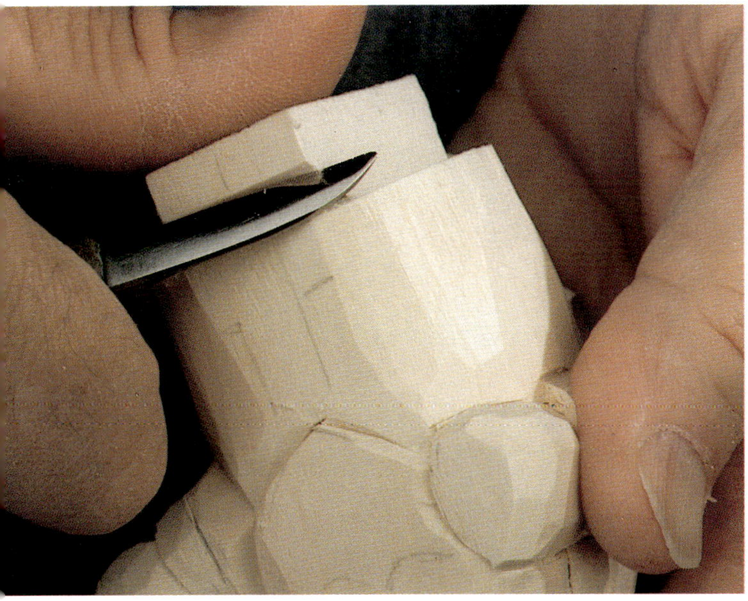

Round the bottom of the robe to give it a little better look.

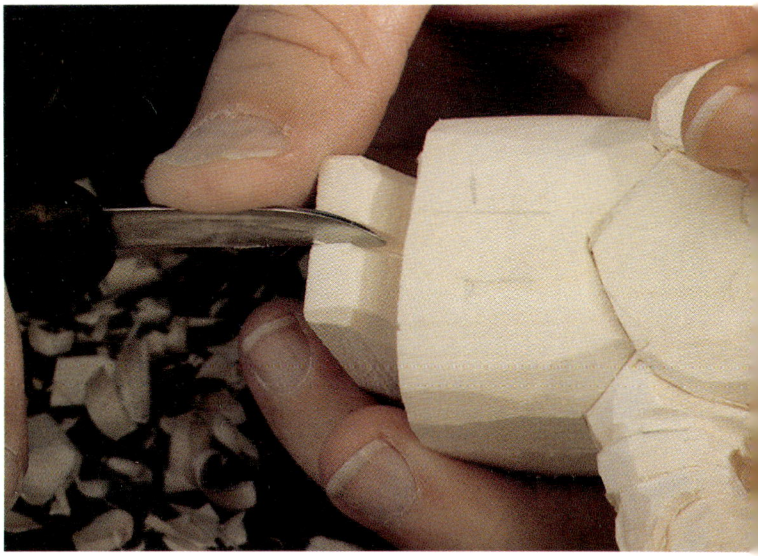

Separate the feet.

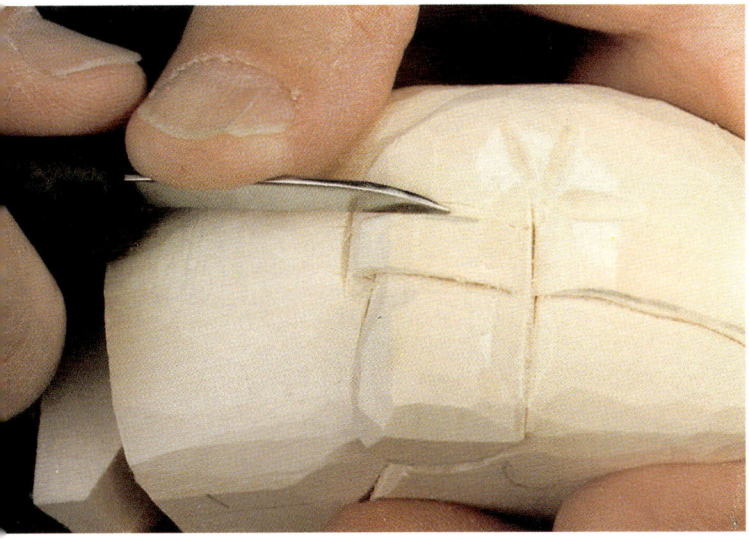

Start cutting in the sleeves.

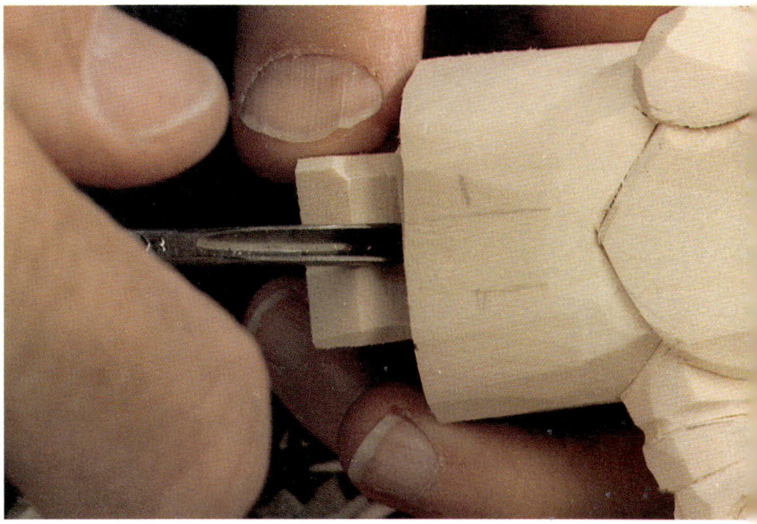

Up here it is difficult to carve with the knife, but this little gouge does the work easily.

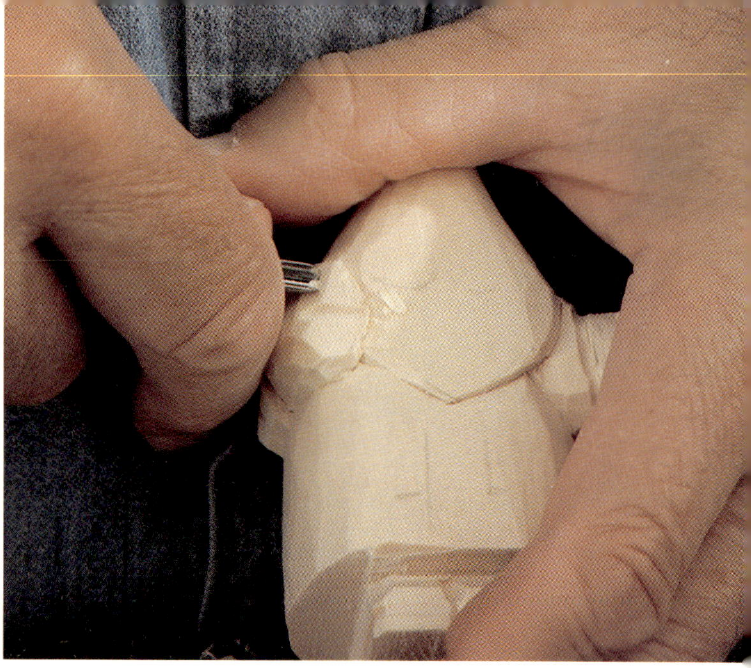

Incise the line of the heels and notch the edges to separate the heels with your knife. On these feet it is not necessary to add the sole with the gouge, but you can if you want to.

It will be easier for Santa to play soccer without his mittens so carve in the fingers with the small gouge beginning with the middle finger and working out.

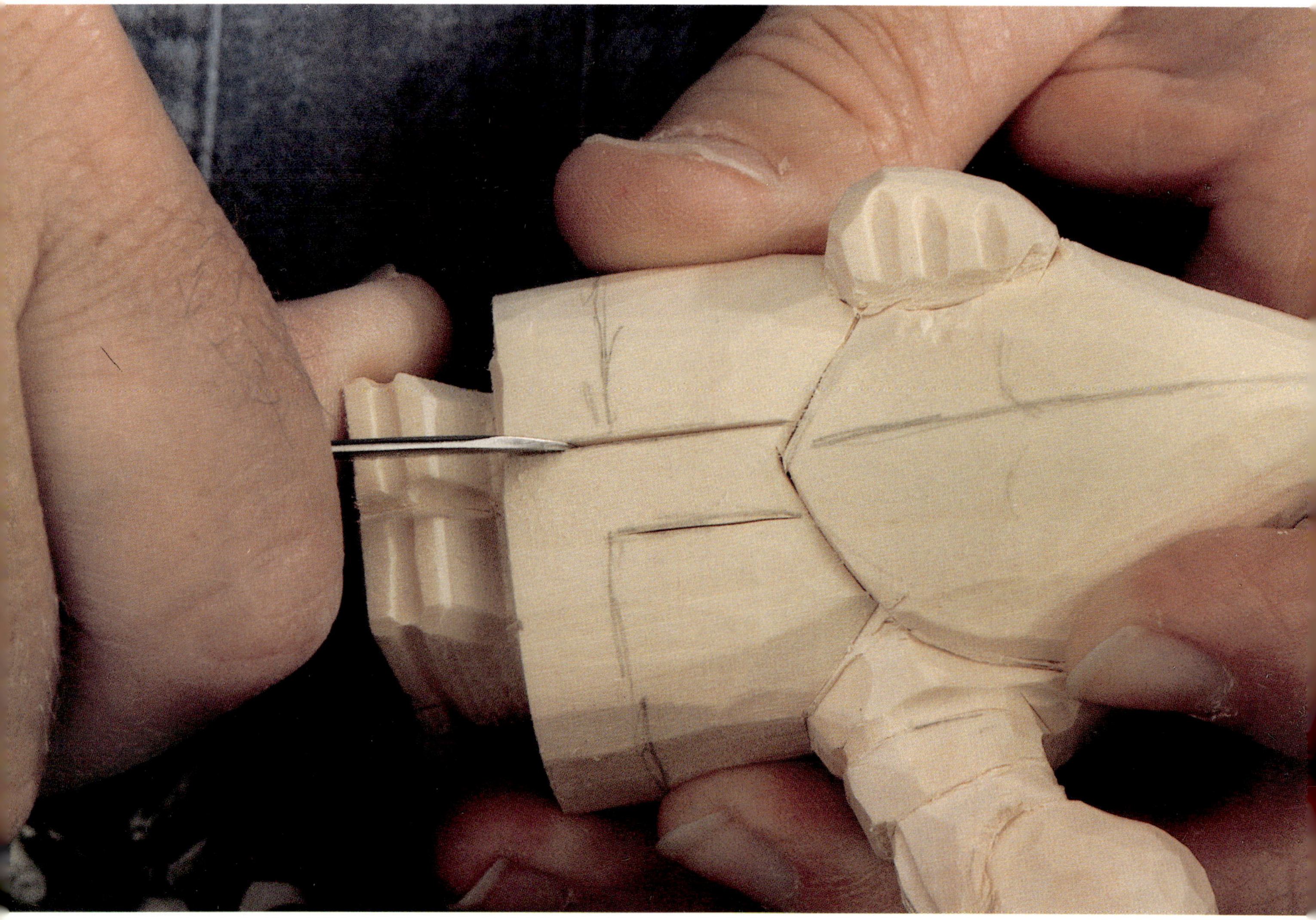

Incise the fur lines on Santa's robe.

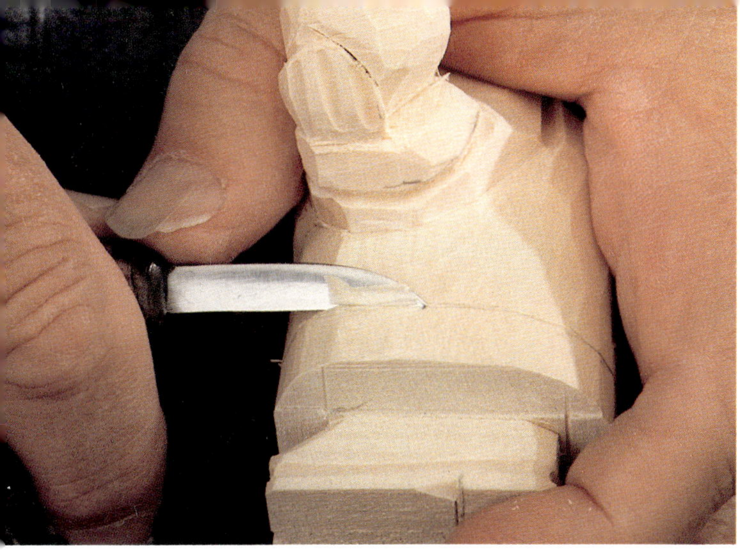

Round down the robe at the edges of the incised fur lines so the fur is raised.

Using the knife incise along each side of the nose.

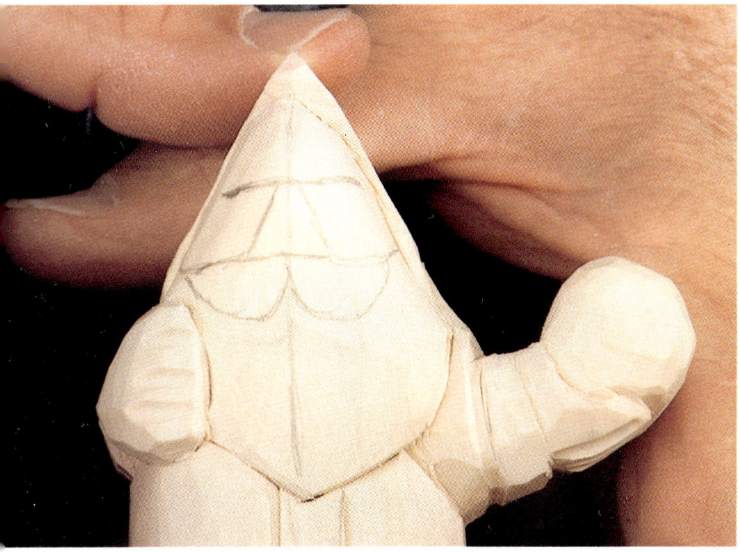

Draw in the face, first drawing in a center line as a guide.

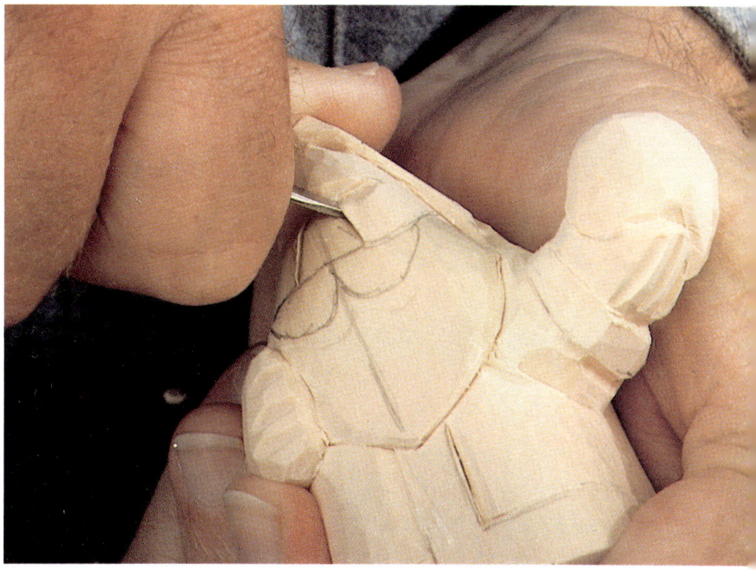

Turn the Santa over to incise the other side of the nose.

Rock your knife deeply into the eye channel and then remove a nice sized wedge for the eyes.

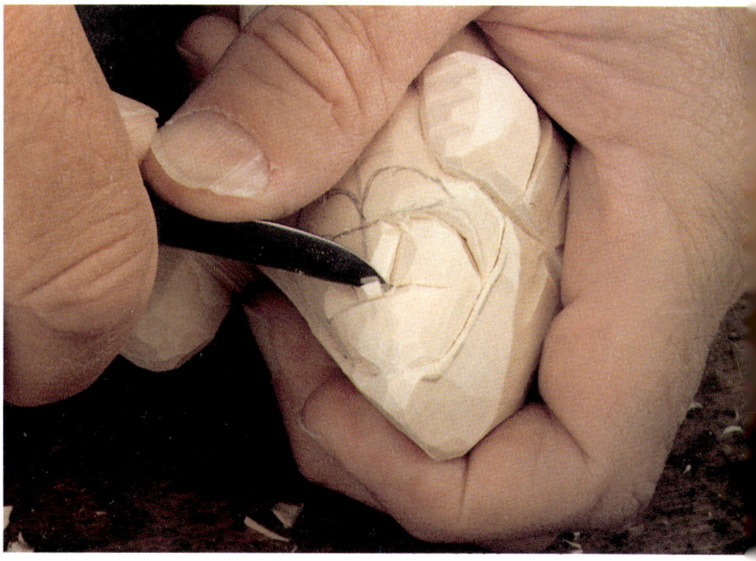

Trim up the sides of the nose and start rounding the cheeks into the mustache and beard.

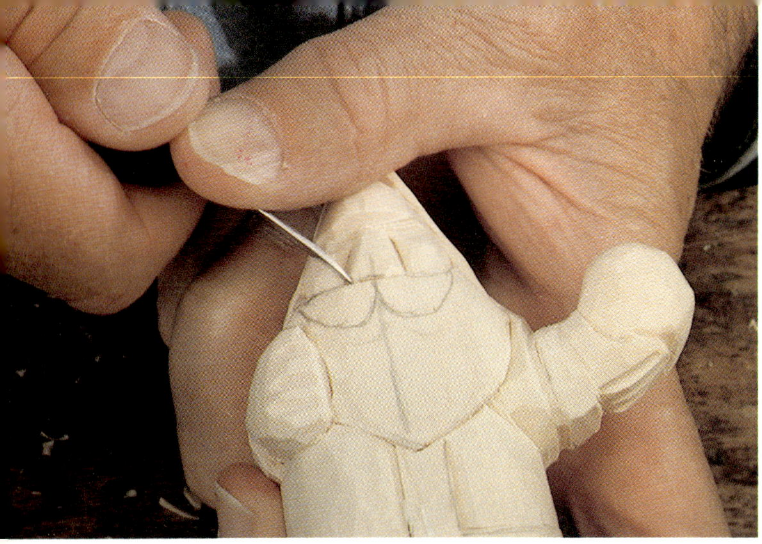

Be sure to carve off a little of each side of the nose for the nostrils.

Cut in the eyebrows with a nice gentle cut, not too deep.

Cut in the mustache and trim out below it.

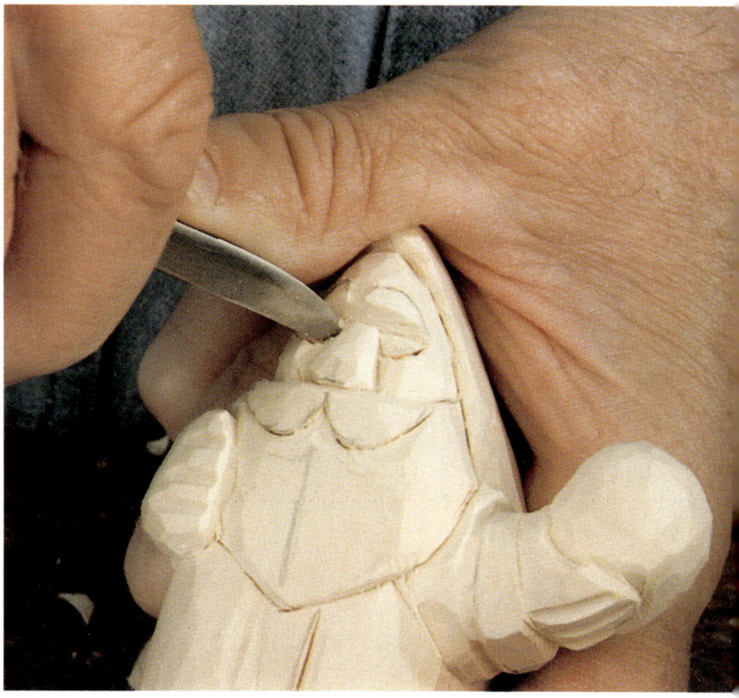

Put in a nice deep cut one each side of the eye.

Carve in an oval look on the eyeballs.

I think the boxers outfit would work well with this soccer player. You could also leave the hood off and show the hair.

Baseball Santa

On the bat, start by cutting a little stop cut with the knife.

Transfer the pattern for the baseball playing Santa to your basswood and cut out your blank.

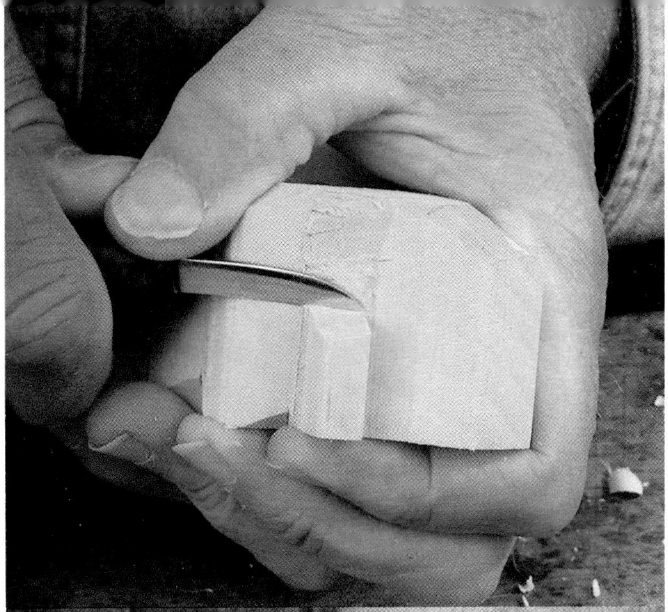

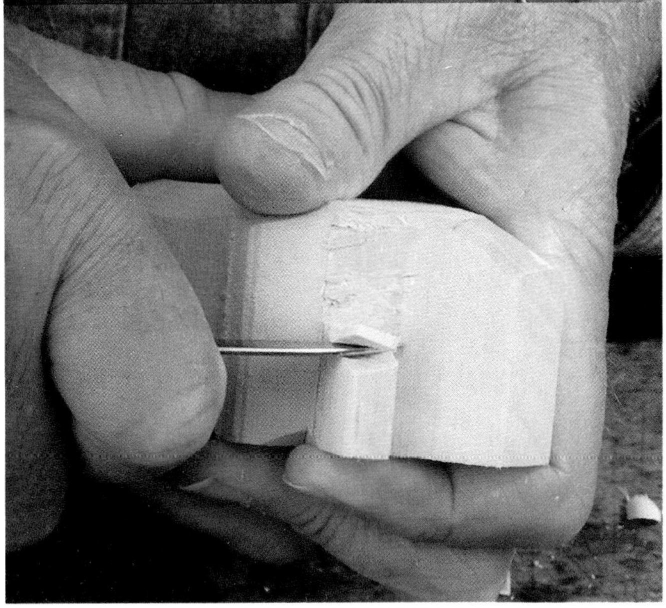

Make small vertical and horizontal cuts until you have the bat down to the size you want it.

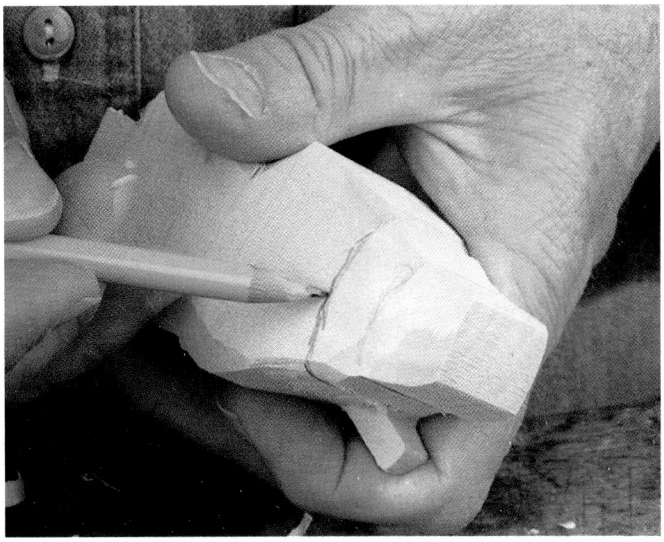

This boy's going to have some hair. Draw in where the hair and hat will be.

Trim down the back of his hair and baseball cap now. They are way too big.

Incise your line all the way around the baseball cap.

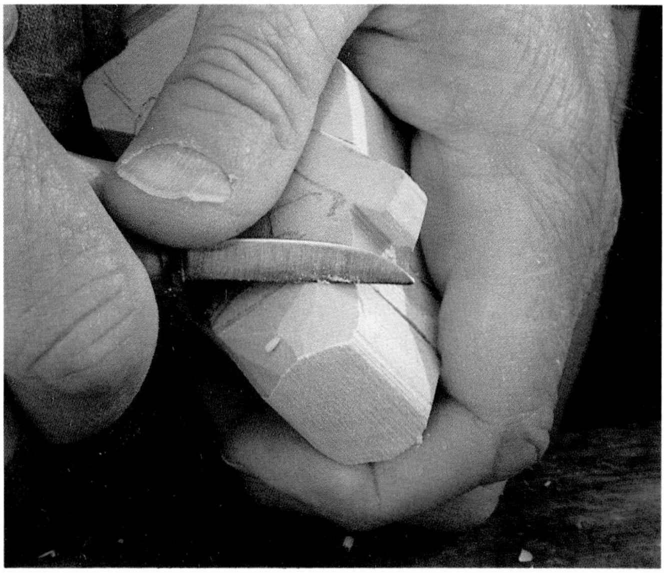

The front of the cap is a little to big. Take off some of that as well.

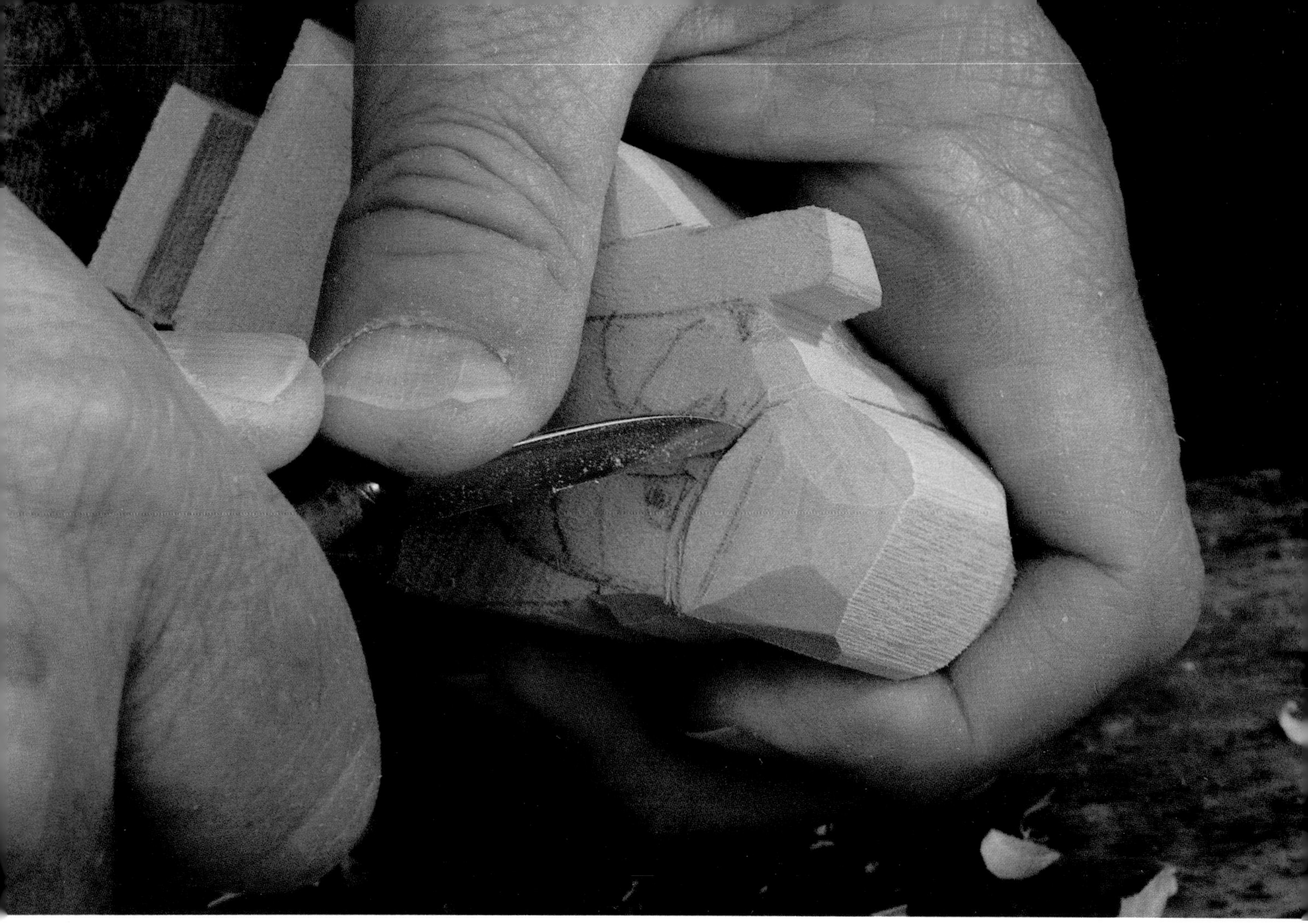

Incise the bill of the cap.

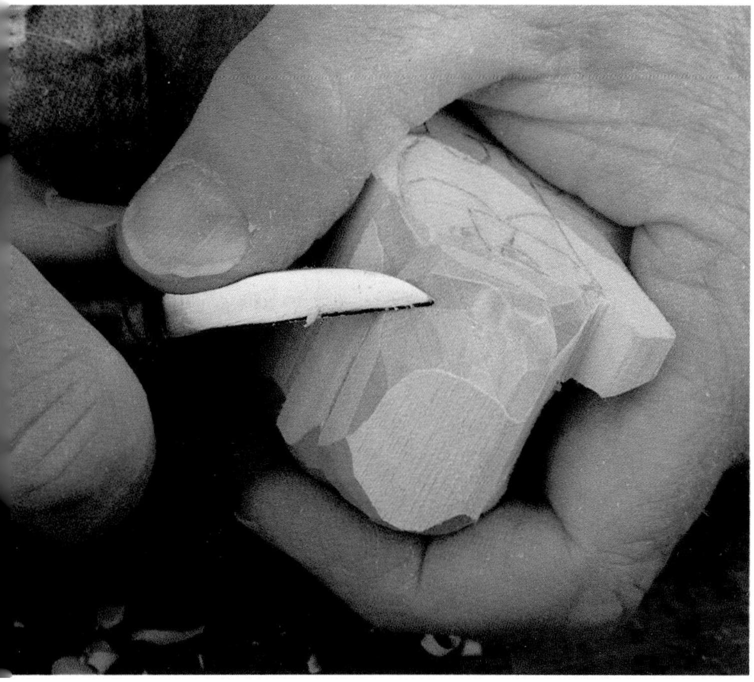

Cut back from the bill of the cap. Continue to cut away until you get the shape of the rest of the cap.

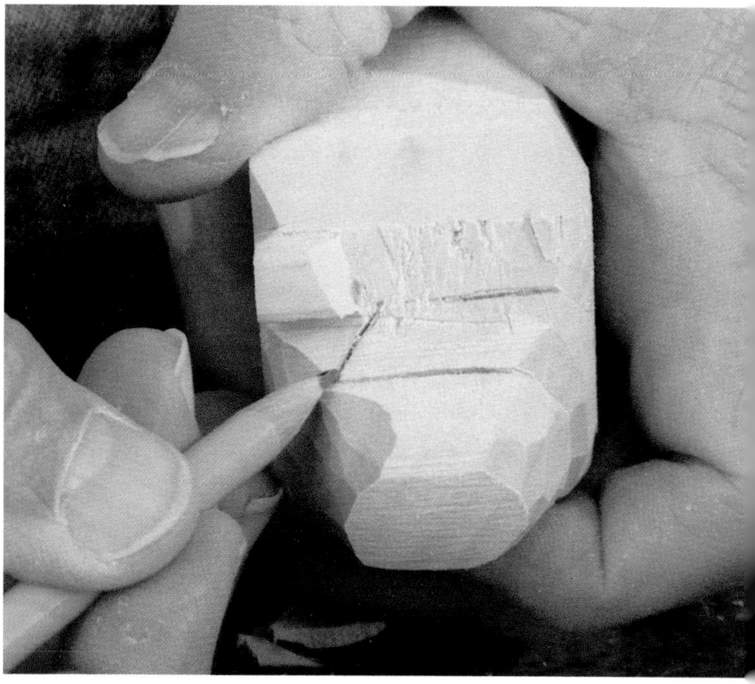

Decide where you think the hair should go on both sides of the head and mark it in with a pencil.

Cut the area in front of the hair out.

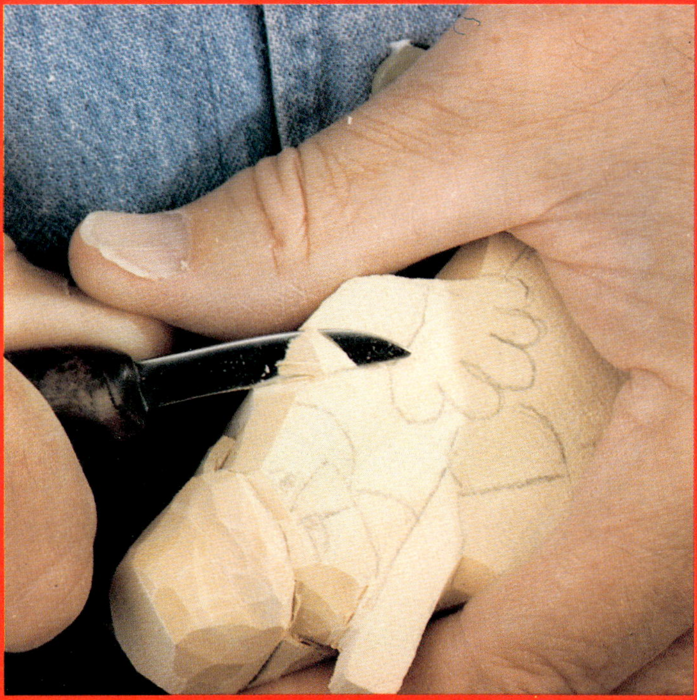

Start working the left arm into the beard.

Blend the top of the hairline under the hat.

Continue defining the arm up to the hair.

Cut in the backs of the arms with two big V cuts.

Use the small gouge to define the lower part of the arm holding the bat on the side view.

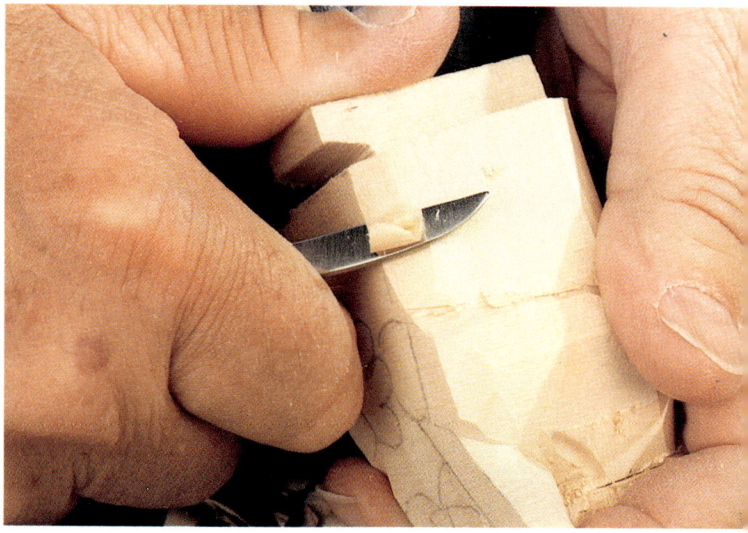

Round down the front of the robe.

Incise the bat, Santa's hand and his glove.

I've cut out around the glove and will shape it as needed as I go.

Begin rounding and tapering the bat.

Continue to cut away from the baseball glove.

This is a real close place I was having trouble getting my knife into. I'm using a Dremel MINIMITE to reach it. Some people think they're cheating when they use power tools. Personally I don't care if you gnaw it off to get down to the point where you can put in the detail.

Cut away from around the bat.

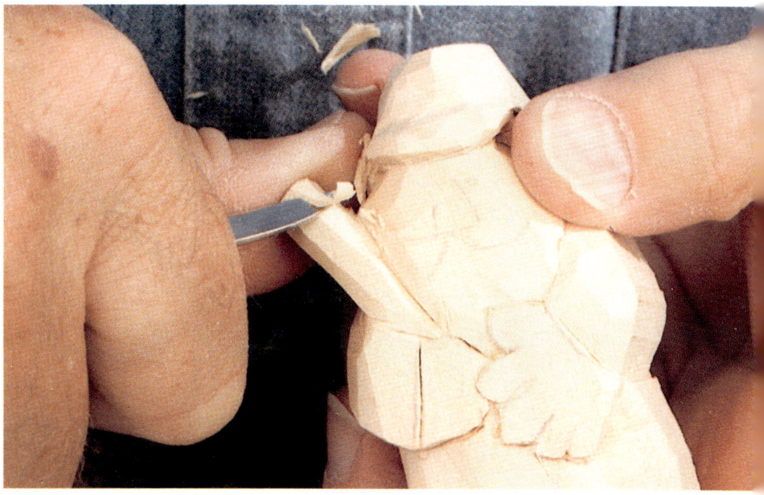

Continue rounding down the bat and defining the edge of it where it meets Santa's beard.

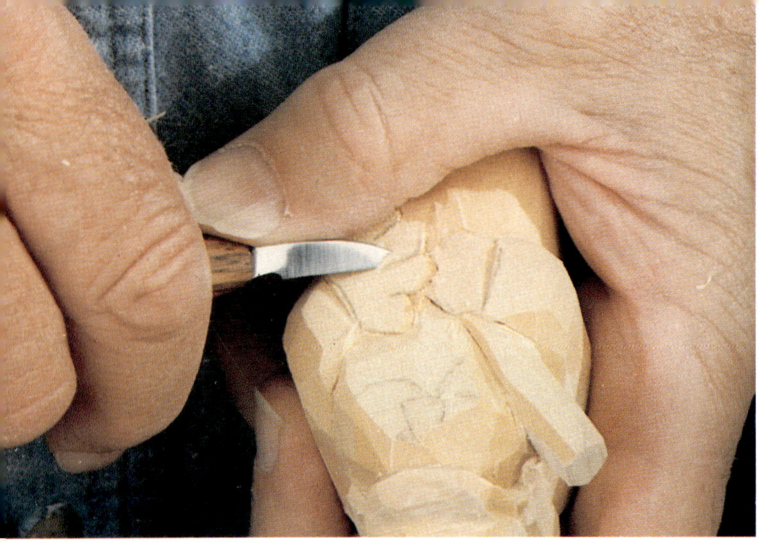

This is obviously an "old-timey" baseball glove, but I'm working here to give it some shape around the fingers.

Put in fingers on this hand with a small gouge, beginning with the middle finger and working out.

Carve out this little space along the back of the glove.

Cut in the small triangles to represent the heels and use the small gouge to cut in the soles.

I've decided the arm needs to be cut a little deeper around the beard.

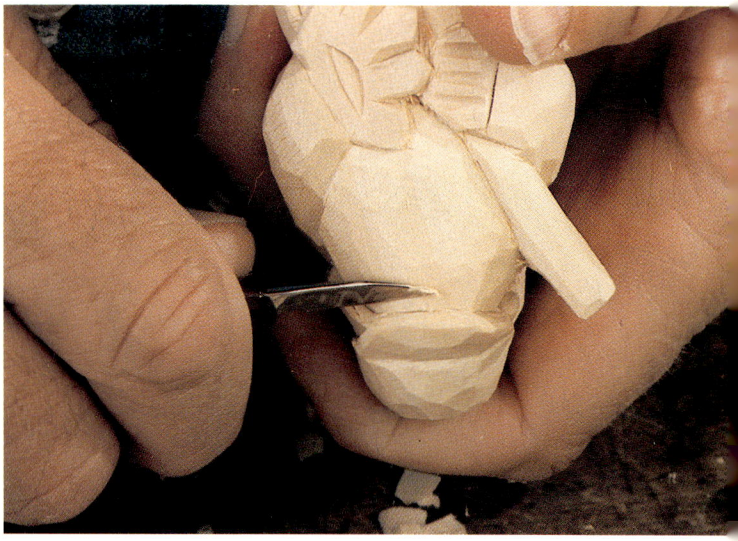

Round in the area of the face. This is a pretty close area for a face but we're going to do it. Cut back in under the bill to give the hat a little more definition.

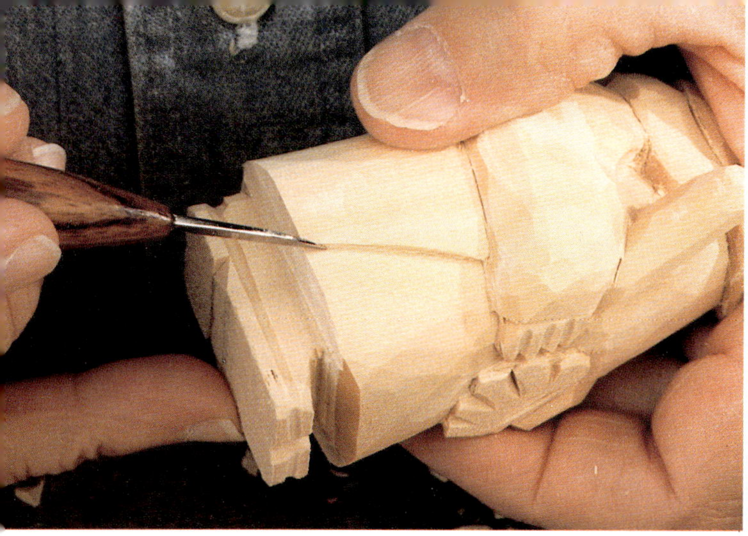

Use your knife to cut away the robe as well.

Cut in the eye channel.

Draw in the center line and Santa's face.

Incise along either side of the nose.

Round the cheeks.

Cut in the mustache.

Cut off the small outer corners of the nose for nostrils.

Cut out two semi-circles for the eyes and with a very light touch, using only the tip of your knife, carve in the eyebrows.

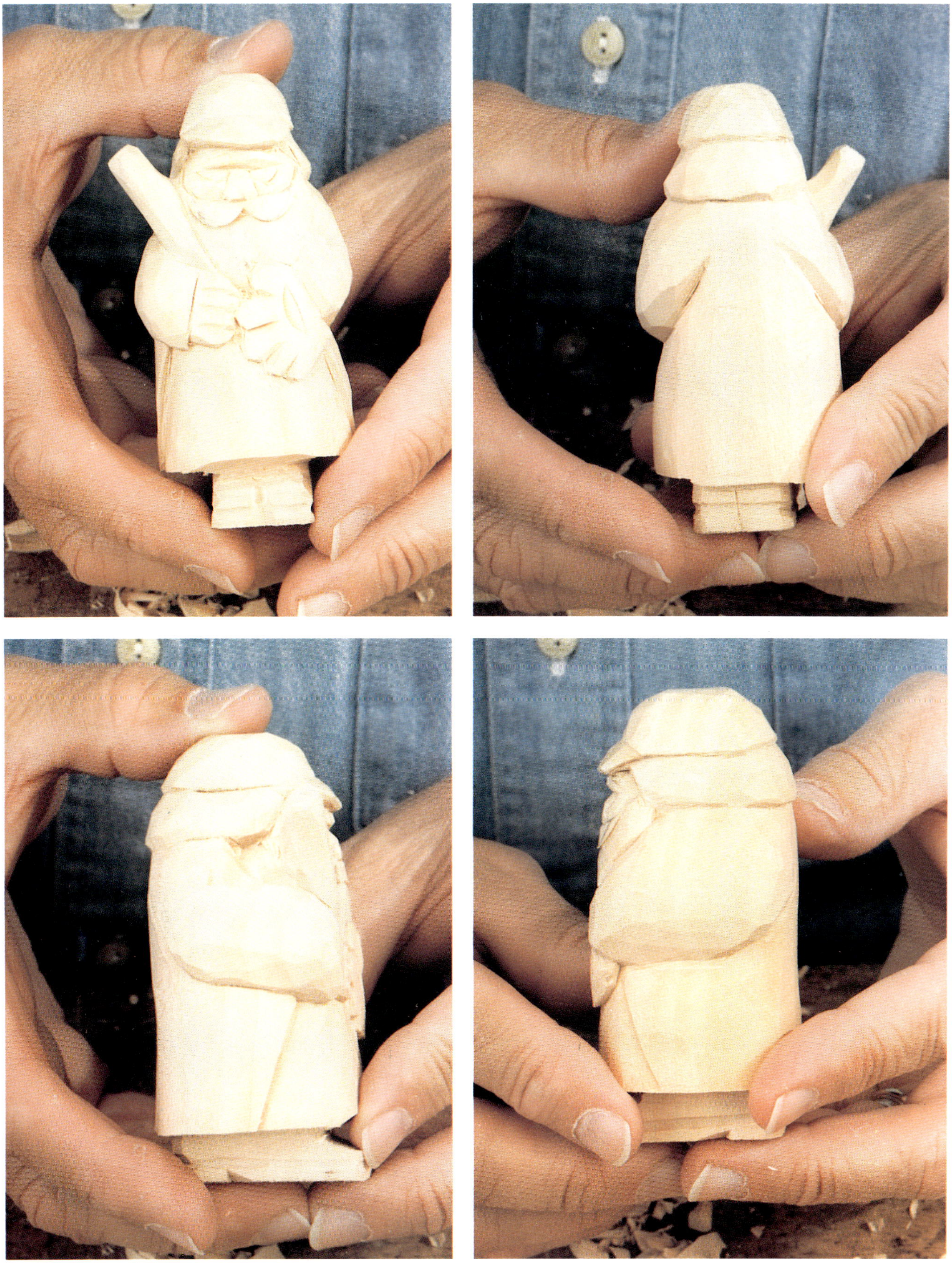

The baseball playing Santa. Everybody on your softball or baseball team will want one of these Santas. Be sure to price it fairly for yourself.

Santa Holding Tree

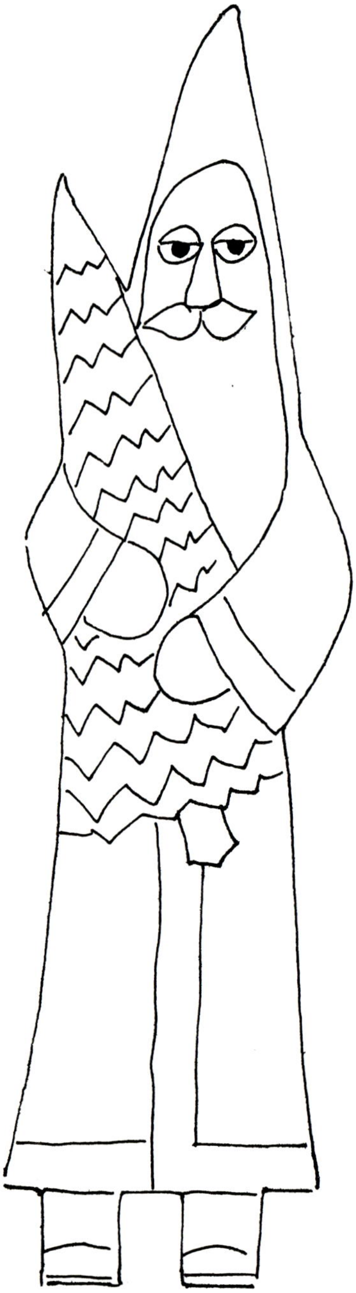

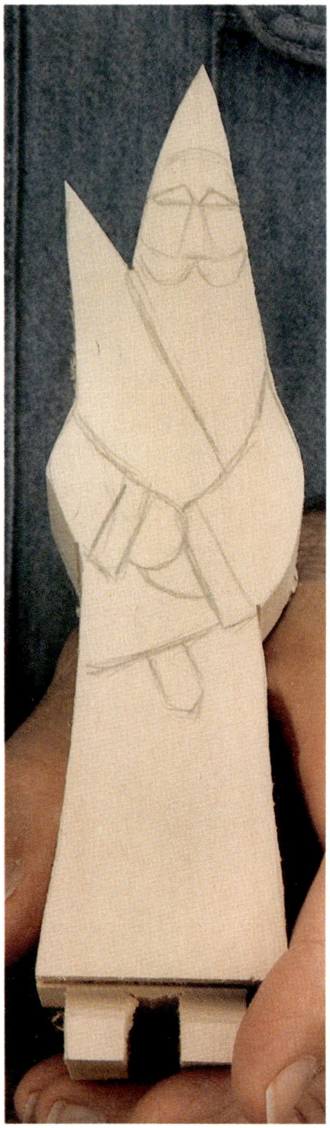

We're finished with the sporting Santas. Now we're going to do a more traditional Santa holding a tree. This works well for the long, narrow scraps I occasionally produce. Transfer the pattern to the block and cut it out with a band saw.

Cut out the waste around the tree. A knife or gouge will do the trick. Or, as we said before, gnaw it off if you like.

Working the right sleeve into the tree.

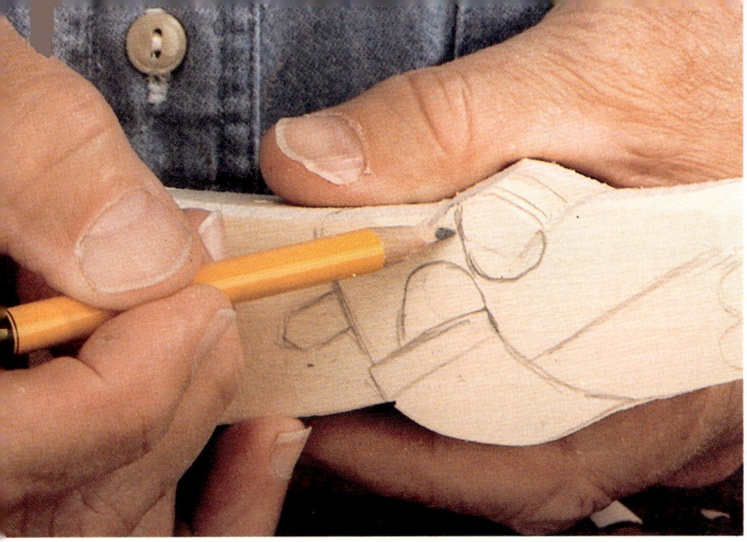

We all make mistakes. I don't like the looks of this hand. So, I'm going to erase it and try again. As I've said many times, this pencil is one of your most useful tools. It's done wonders for my golf score.

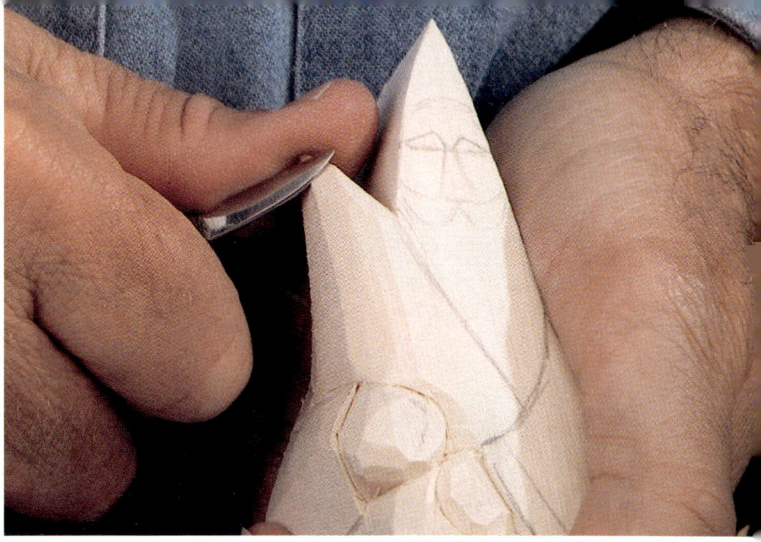

Start rounding and shaping the tree.

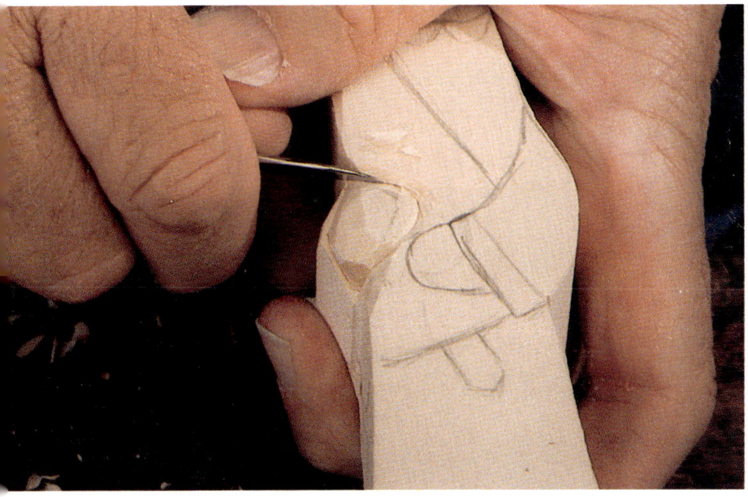

Incise the line of the hand around the tree and shape the hand.

Incise the line where the tree covers the beard.

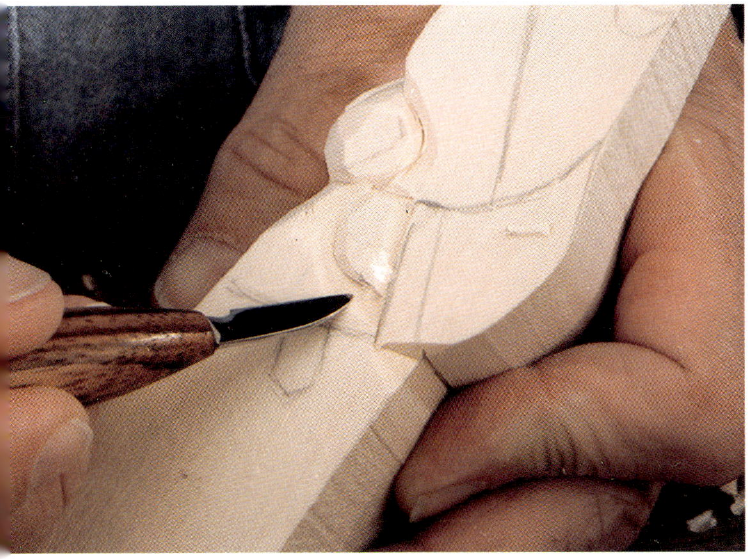

Cut in the other hand. I have the hands almost like I want them now. Cut the hands into the sleeves.

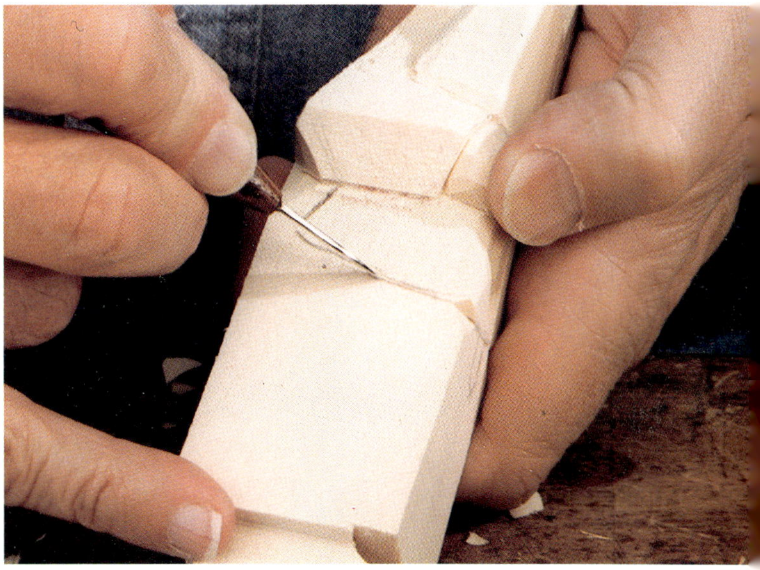

Incise the line of the bottom of the tree.

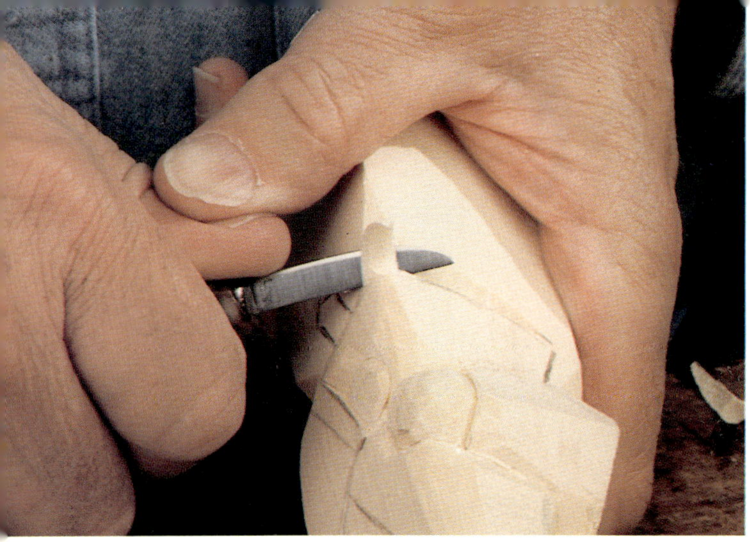

Continue shaping the tree, working wood away from around it's base.

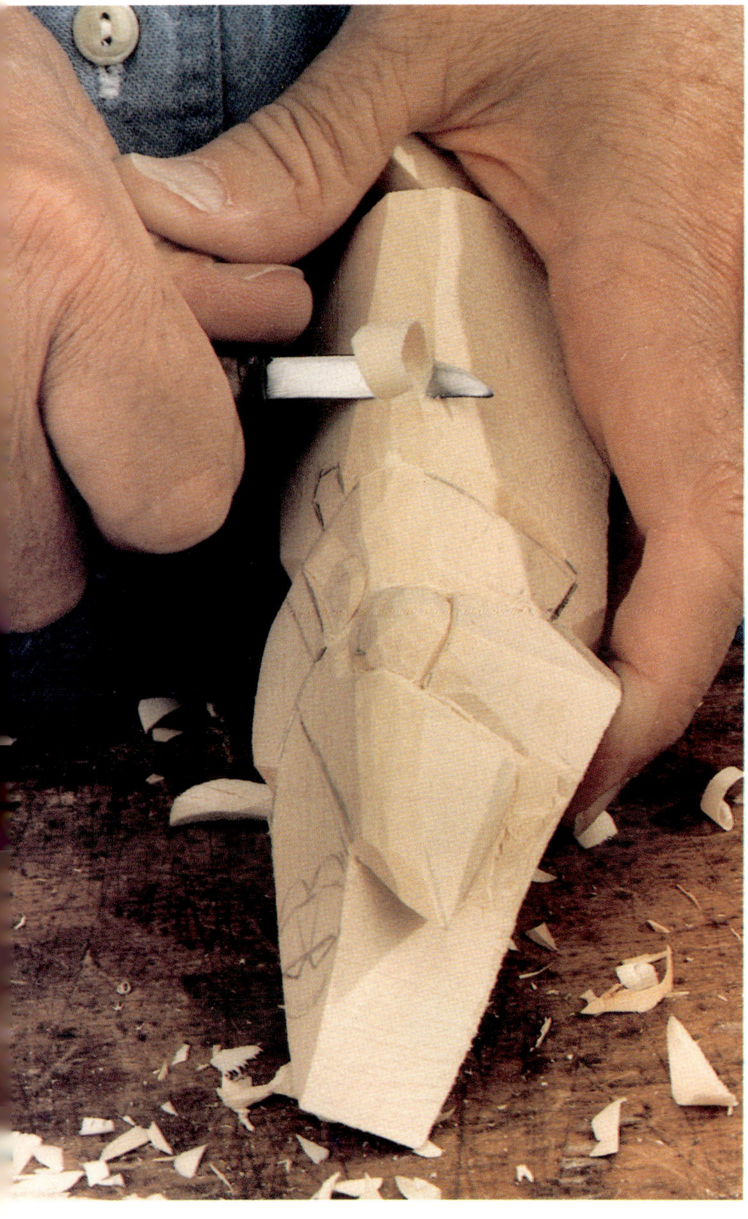

This is a good time to begin rounding Santa's robe. Round each side of the robe.

I'm incising the tree stump. Notice I have the knife in pretty far because we are going to recess this stump quite a bit.

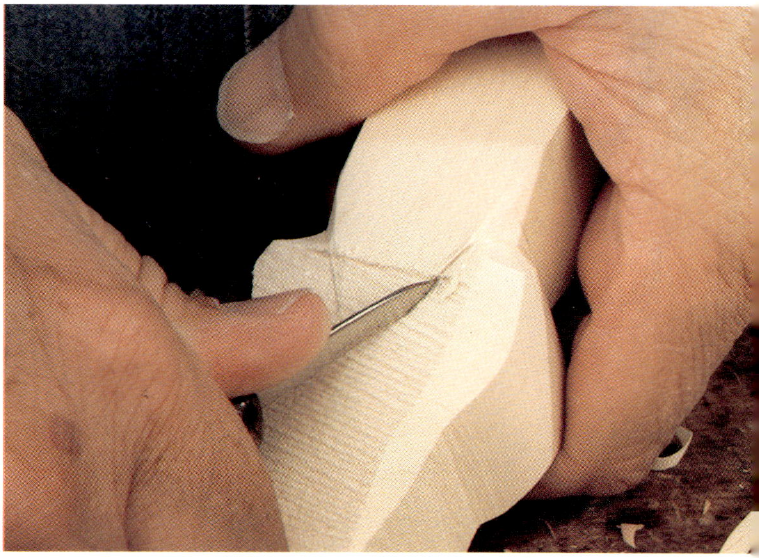

To begin to relieve the back of the arm, put your knife in straight on the line and cut pretty deep.

Then cut in at an angle. This will give you the back of your arm.

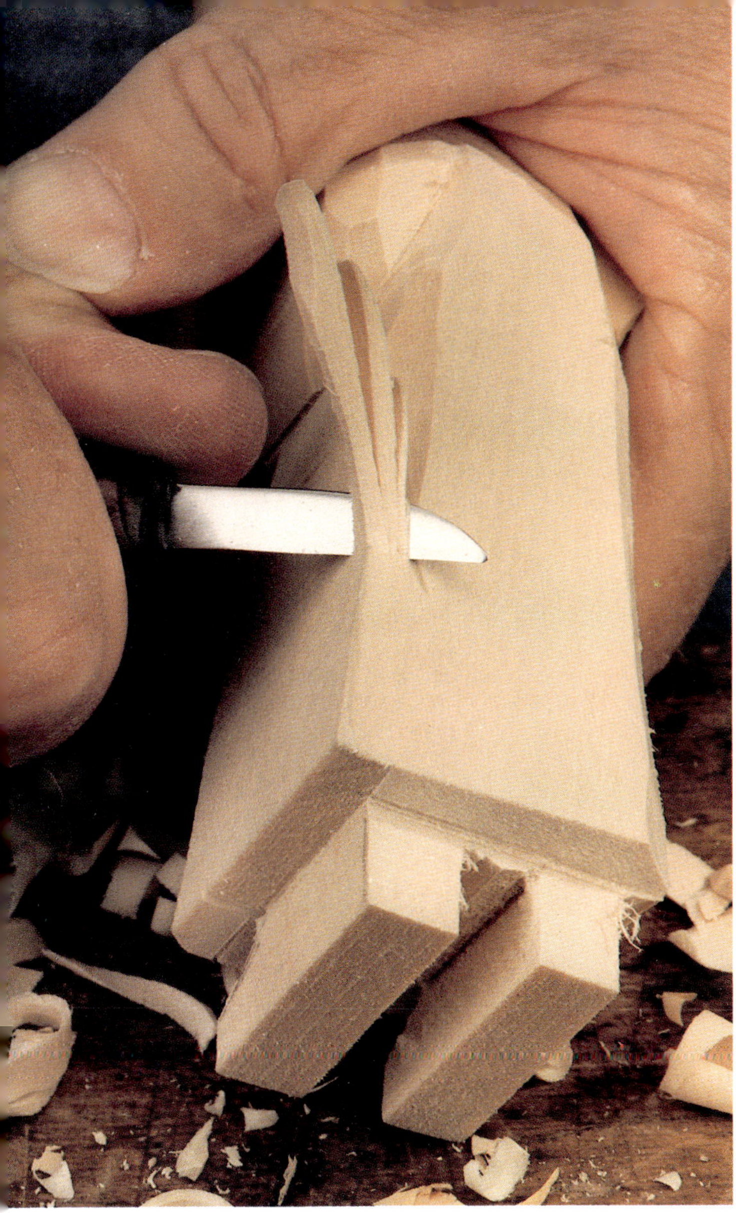

Nip off the sharp edges of the shoes.

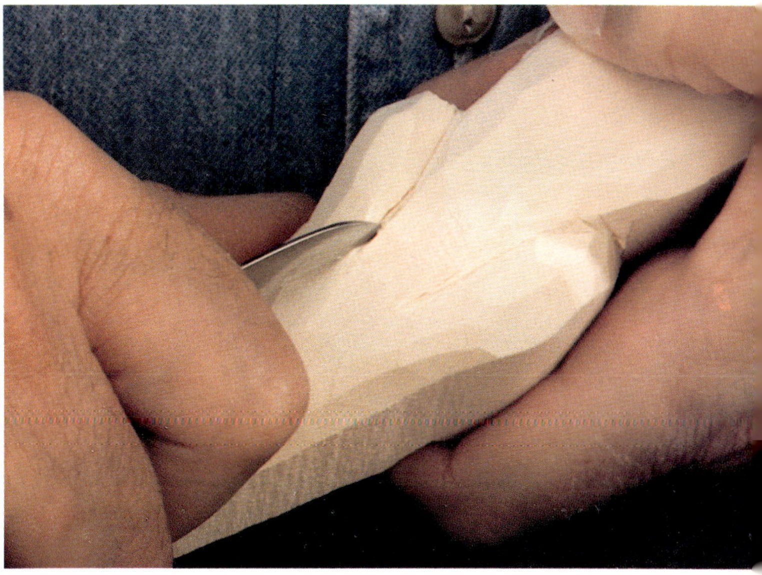

While we're back here we might as well take the sharp edges off the back of the robe.

I'm going further up the back of the arms. I decided they were not long enough.

There was a little excess wood between the feet from the band saw. Remove this with a #7 gouge.

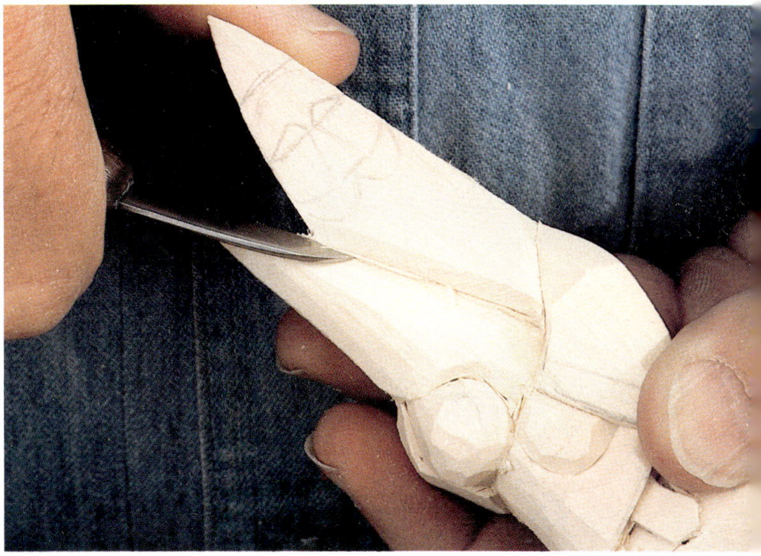

Let's take off some more around the tree next to Santa's beard.

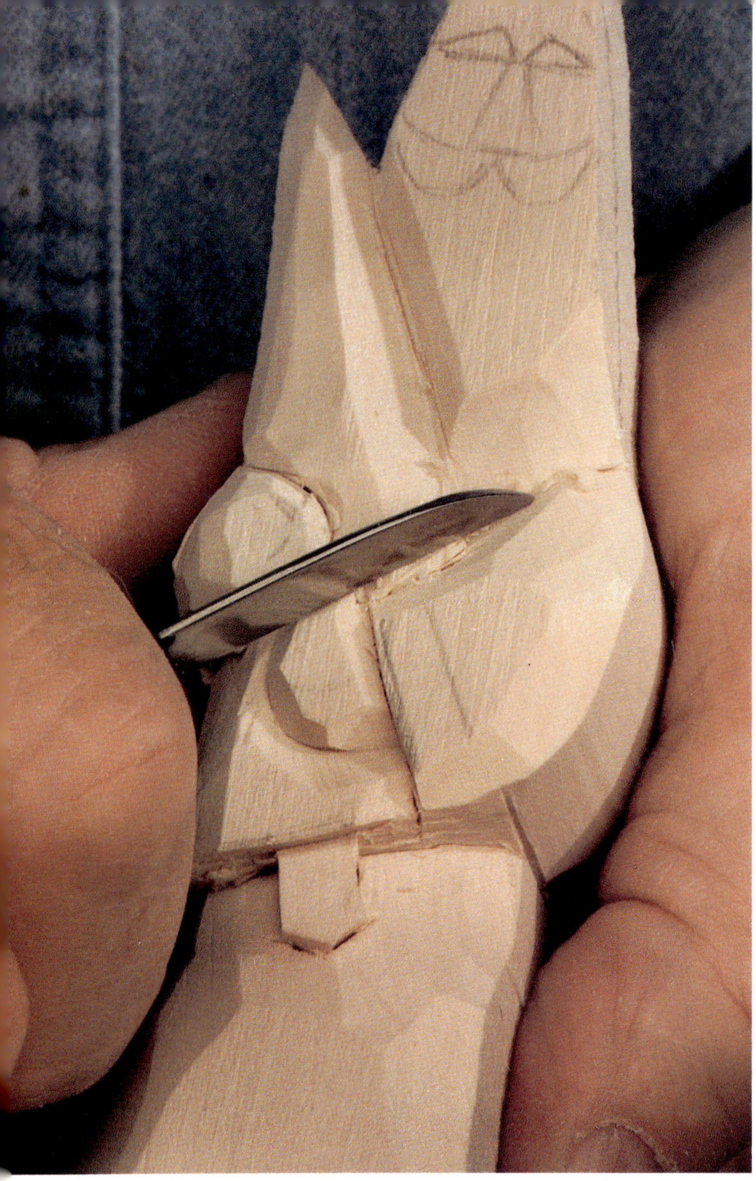

I've rounded some of the left arm away.

Draw in the line around the sides of the face. Cut in your line around the face. You don't have to go too deep as this is a pretty thin piece of wood.

Cut in the sides of the face to your incised line.

Continue to round this tree to a point.

Start rounding the face.

This is going to be a pretty small face, so get your smallest detail knife. Draw in the face.

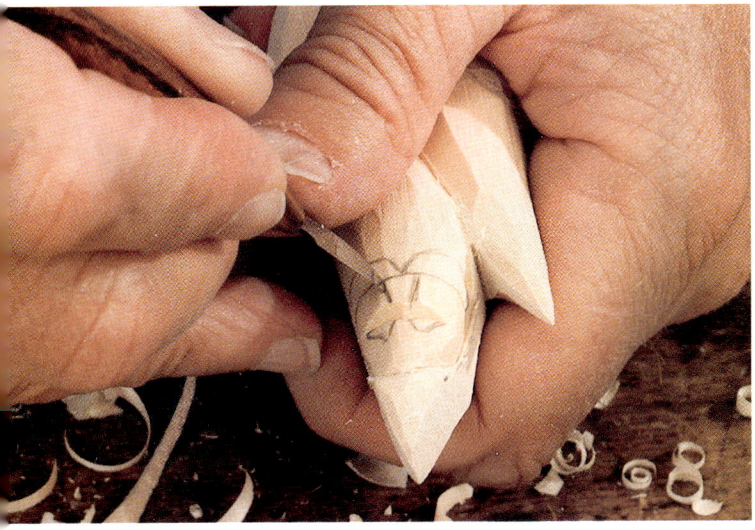

Cut straight in across the eye channel. Cut in at an angle to create a depression for the eyes. Even though this is a skinny little face, you still want to incise along either side of the nose and define it.

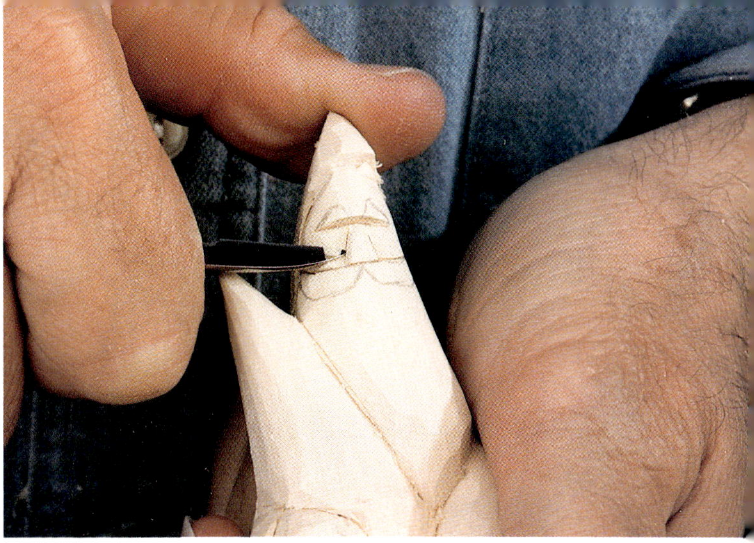

Clean out beside the nose.

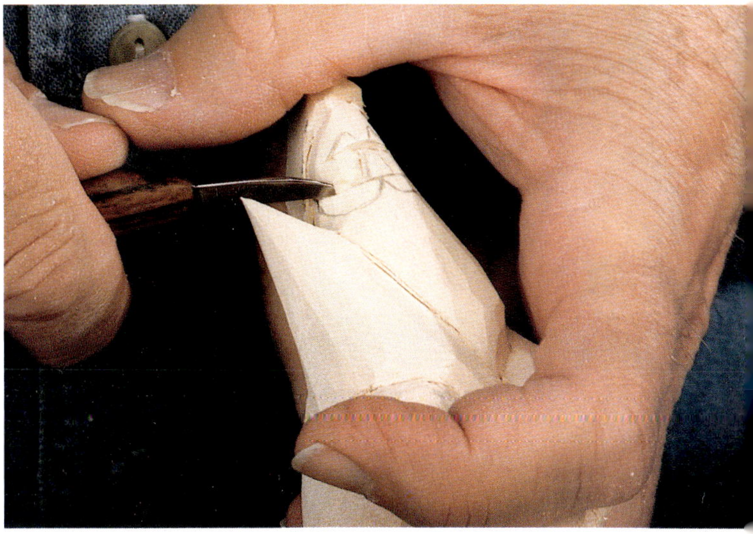

Start rounding the cheek down into the mustache.

It is just as important to clip off the little piece along the outer edge of the nose for the nostril on this small Santa as it is on all the others.

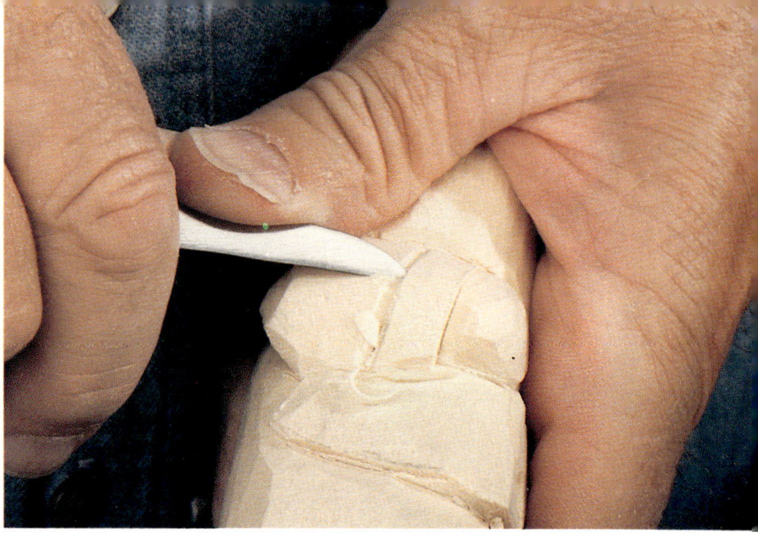

Draw in, incise and relieve all your fur lines.

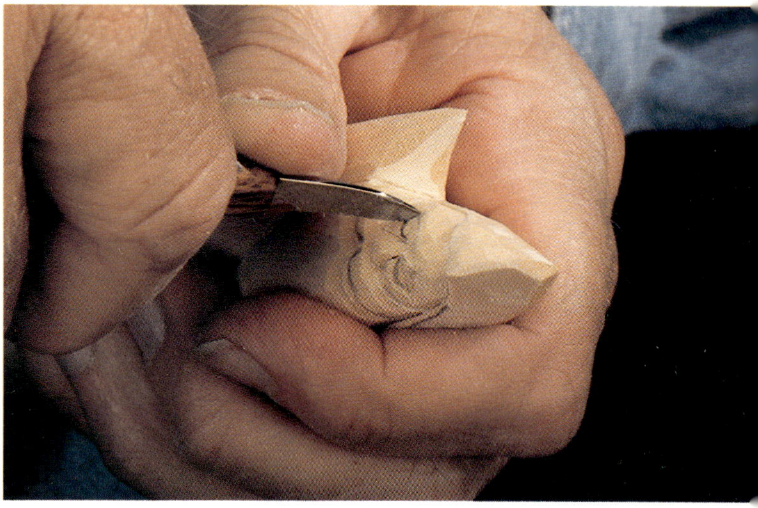

With a face this small you might want to get some magnified glasses available at your local department store to see the fine detail as you work. Shape under the mustache to give it depth.

We're going to do these little eyes the same way we do the large eyes. First stick the blade deeply into the outer corner and then sweep around in a semi-circle.

Carefully cut in his eyebrows.

To give the tree some detail I'm going to put in a series of small zig-zag lines. First draw them in.

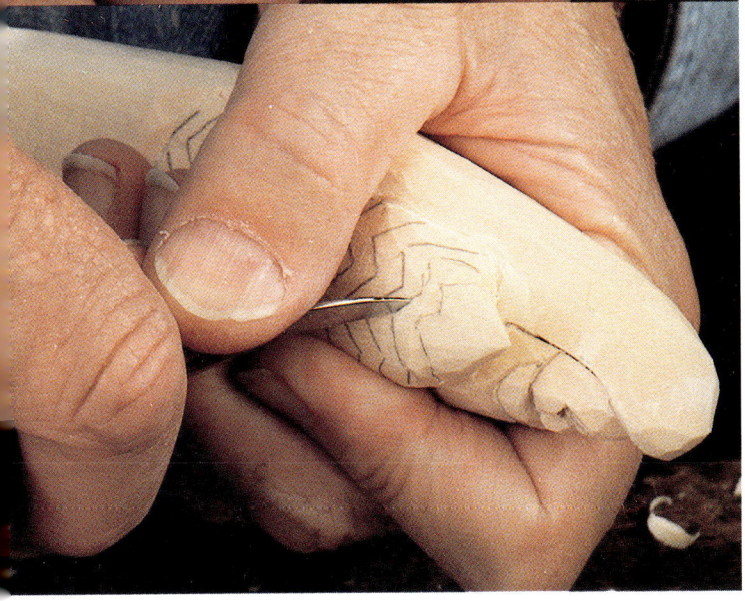

These lines may be burned in with a wood burner or incised and then ...

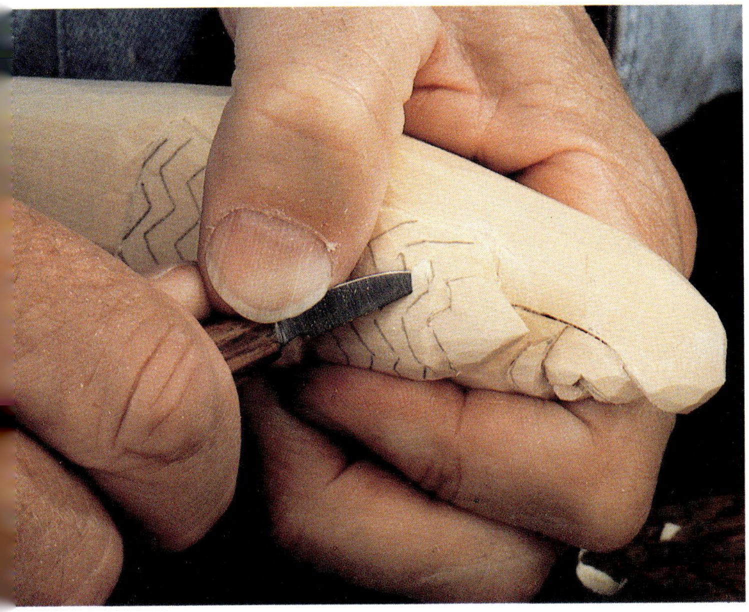

... lay your blade almost on its side and pop out small triangular strips beneath the line to give each tier of branches some depth.

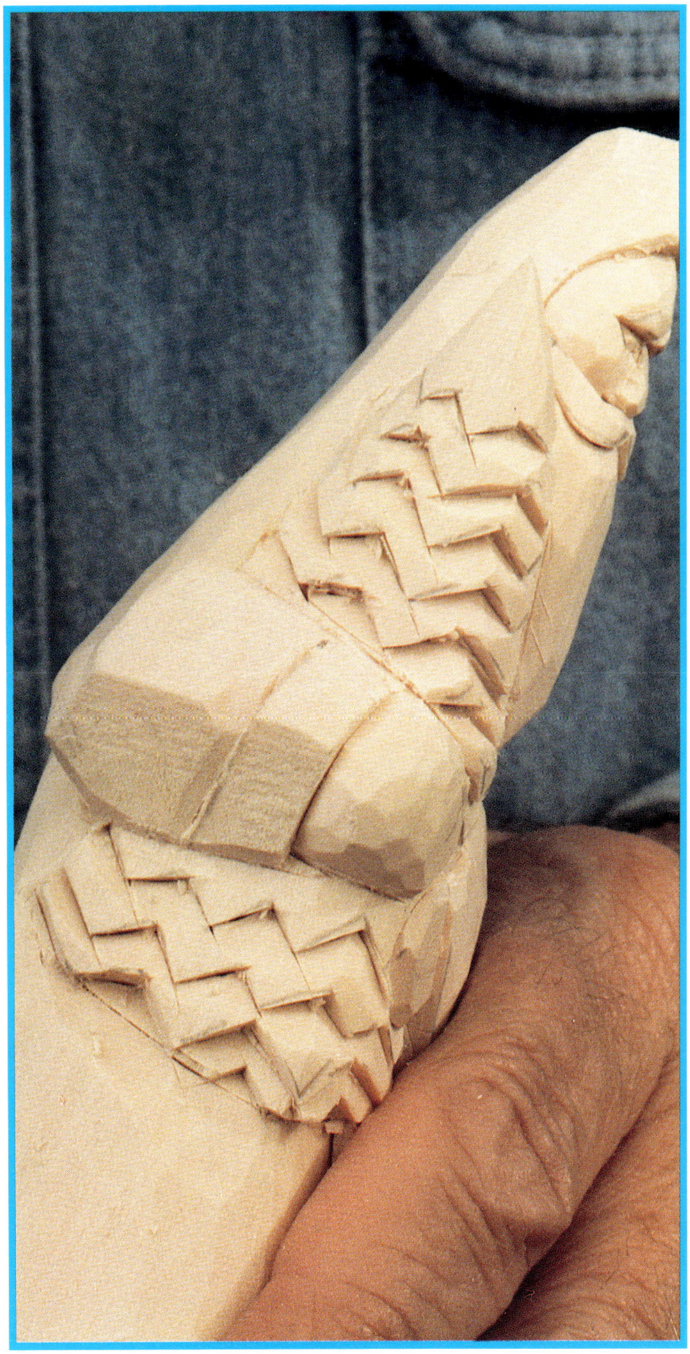

The finished Christmas tree branches.

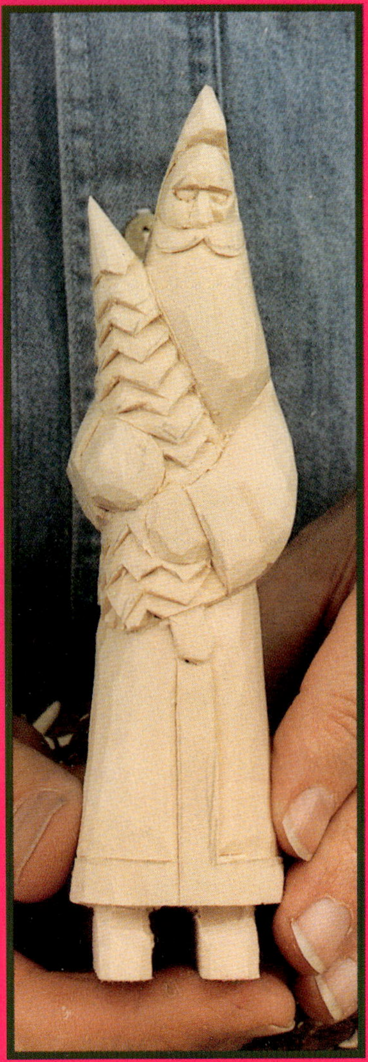
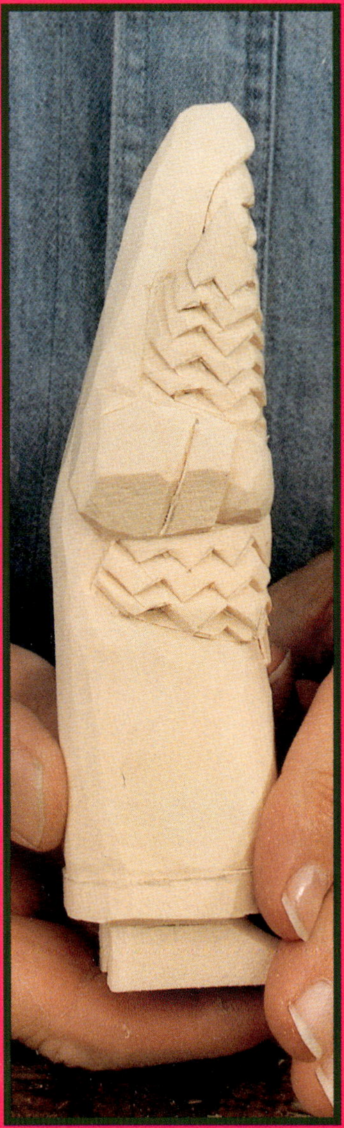
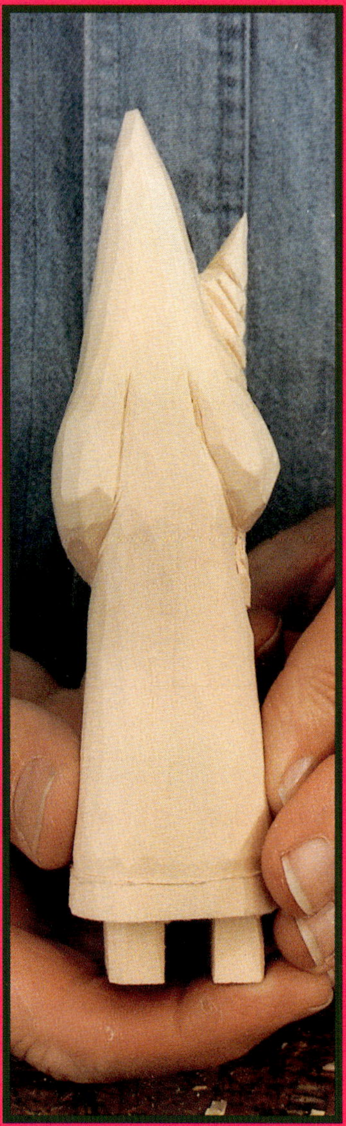
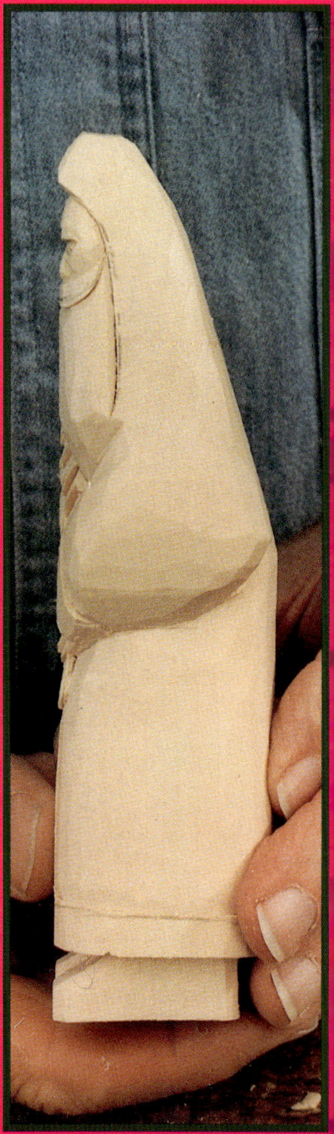

The completed Santa with Christmas tree.

Quilt Santa

I've had a number of requests for a larger version of the quilt holding Santa, so here we go.

Start rounding the backside of the robe. We will not round the front as the quilt will be hanging down there.

To recess the back of the arms a little bit deeper I use the #8 gouge.

Widen the cut with the #5 gouge.

Come back with the knife and clean up the uneven gouge.cuts.

Smooth the back of the robe.

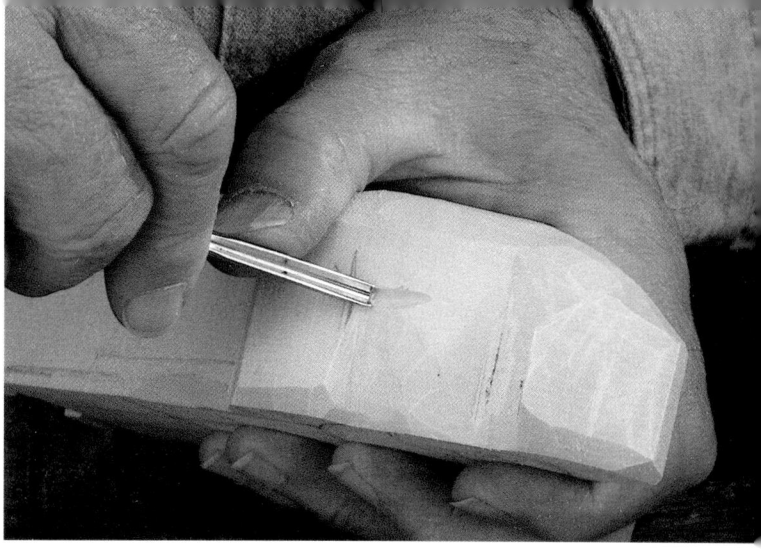

Using a #4 gouge, outline the upper arms.

Now shape the draped over portion of the hood of the robe, both front and back.

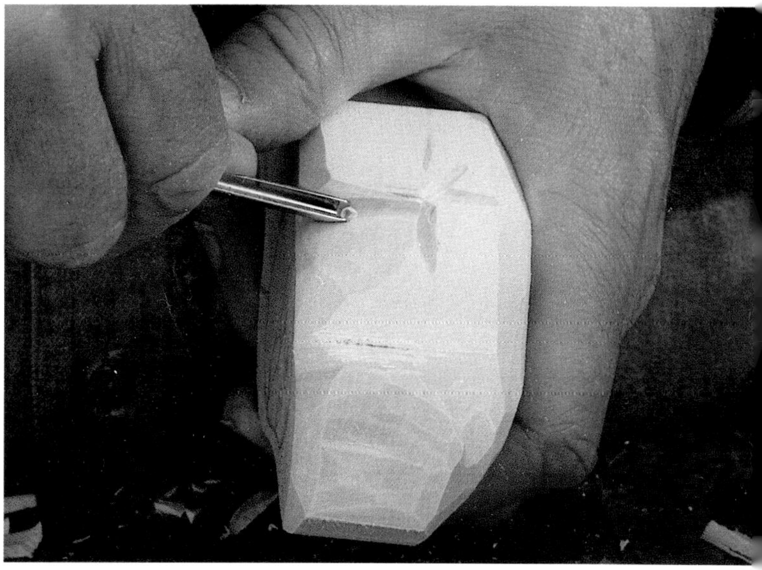

Come back into the area you rounded along the top of the forearm with a #11 gouge.

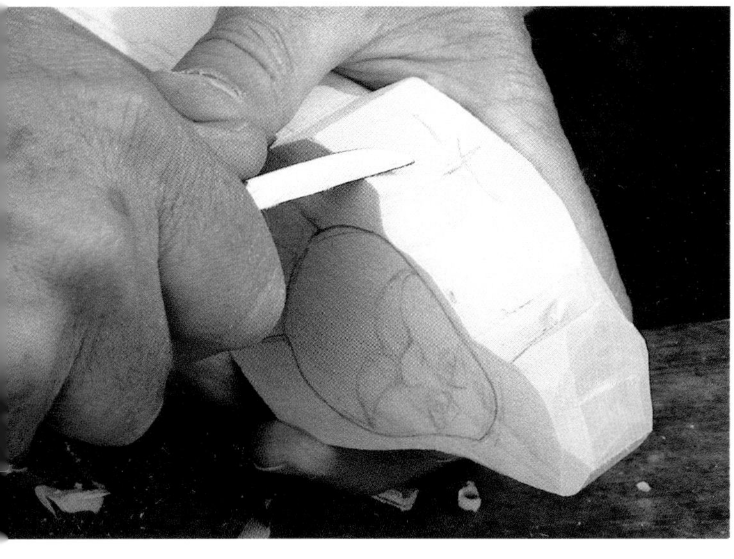

Put in the lines of the arms on the each side and carve a little rounded area to reduce the wood above the arms.

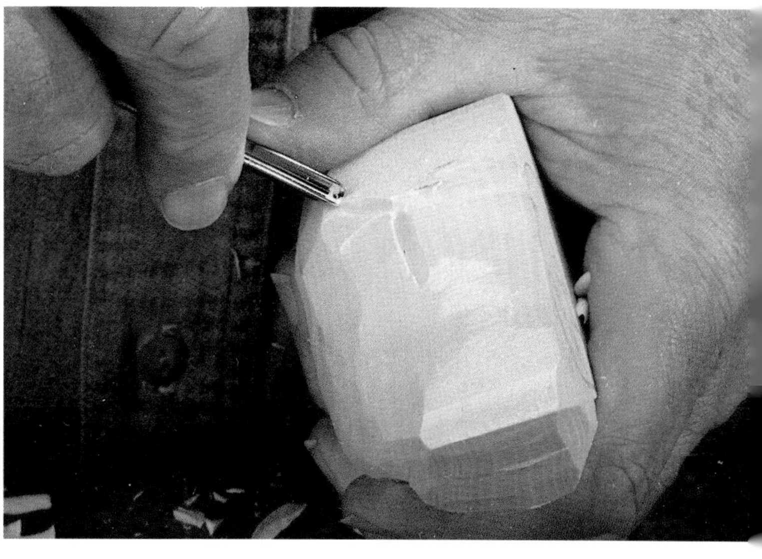

Use the gouge to place creases in the fold of each arm at the elbow.

Follow the line of the quilt out from the front and down along the sides.

The sleeves go under the quilt on each side. Blend them in. The hands are hidden from view beneath the quilt.

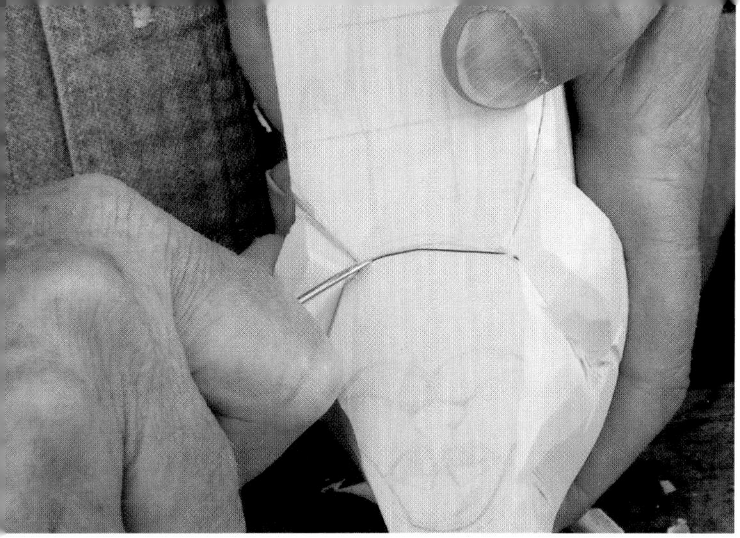

Incise the line where the bottom of the beard and top of the quilt meet. Undercut to give the beard some depth.

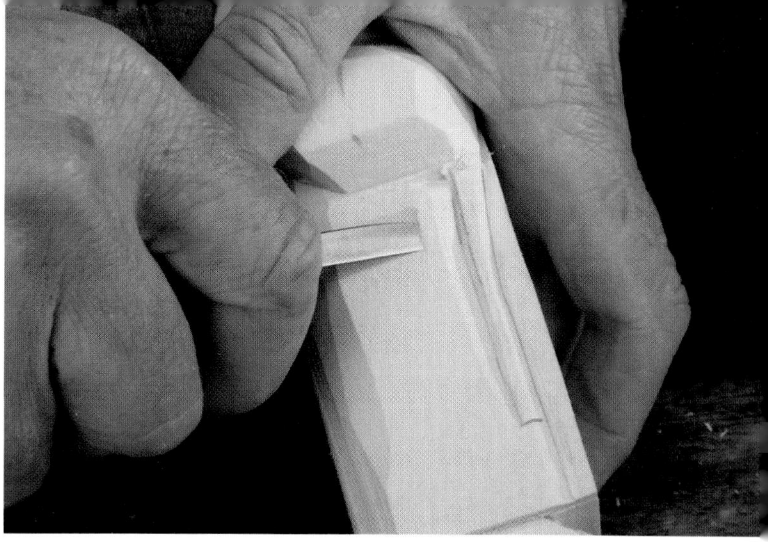

Round the robe in behind the back of the quilt.

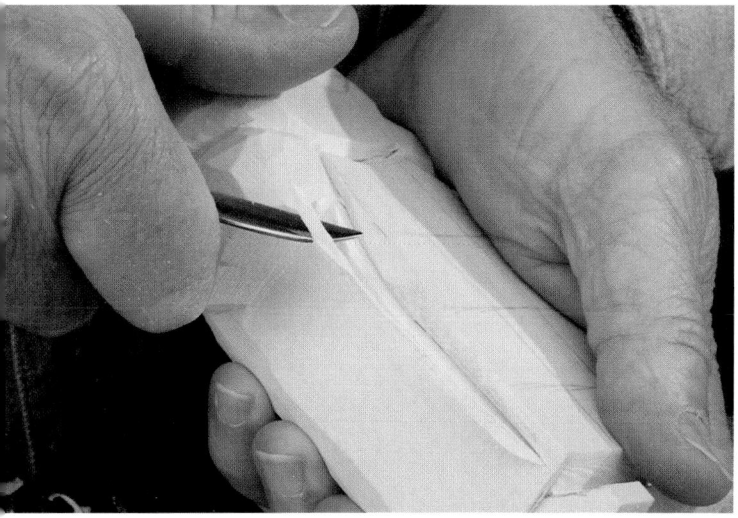

Undercut and remove a strip of wood from along the back edge of the draped quilt.

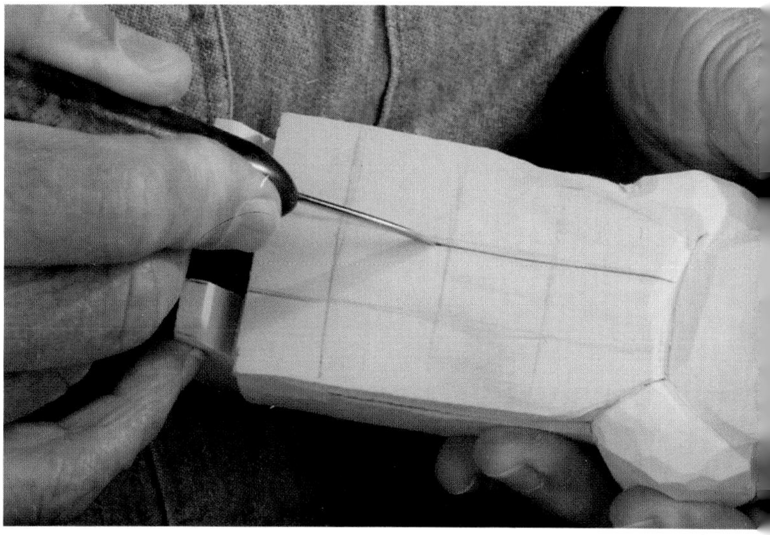

Score the lines for the patterns on the quilt. If the carver is of a mind to, he or she can put in some fancy patterns.

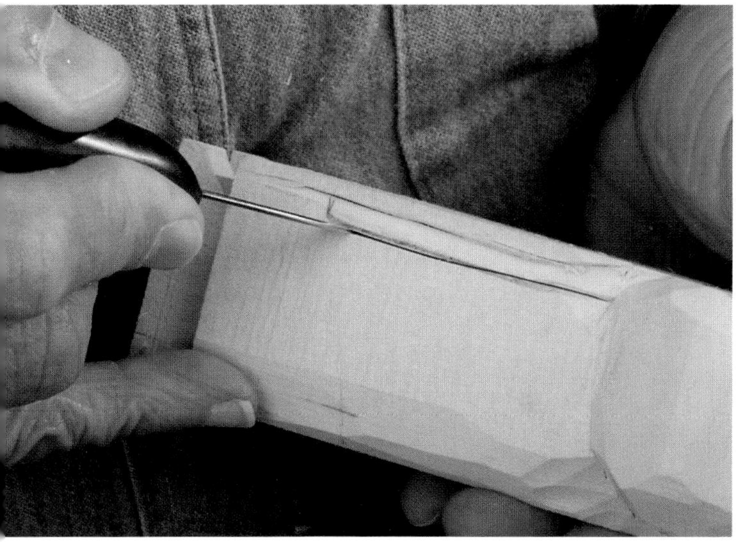

Remember that this quilt is thrown over Santa's arms. So draw in the line for the back of the draped quilt and incise it. Do this on both sides.

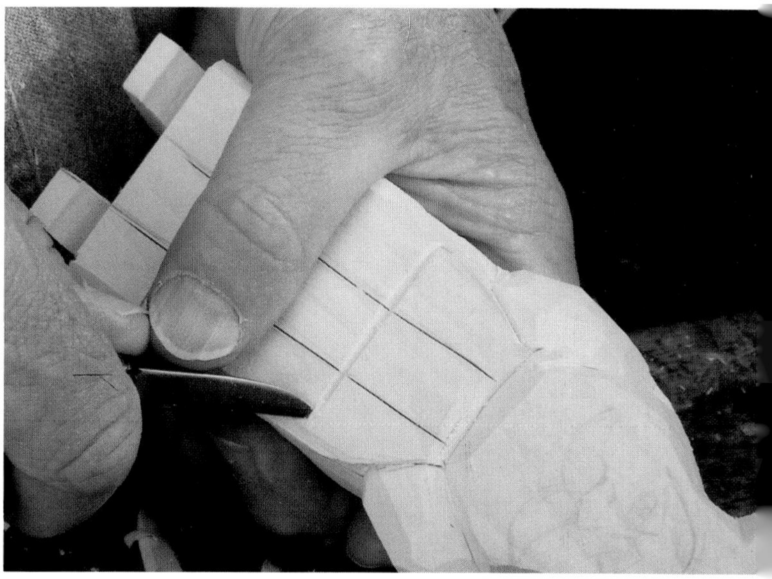

Come back across and make little V cuts on either side of the incised lines to accentuate the pattern ...

... like so.

Use the small gouge to place folds along the top edge of the quilt.

Draw in the areas of the side of the face. This guy's got a wide face, so cut fairly deep when you incise the lines of the face.

Go back along the edge of the quilt lines with a tracing wheel to simulate stitching.

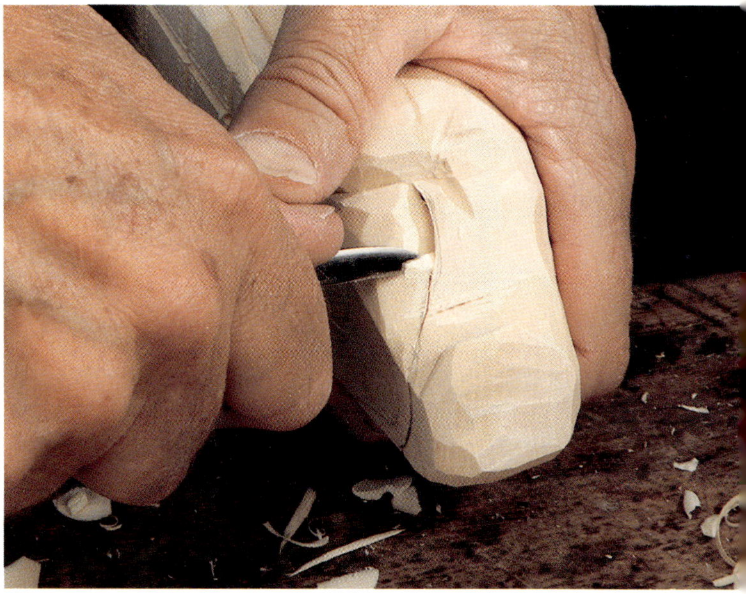

Blend the face back into the incised line beneath the hood.

Round the face.

Cut in the eye channel. Make it a nice deep cut.

Draw in the face.

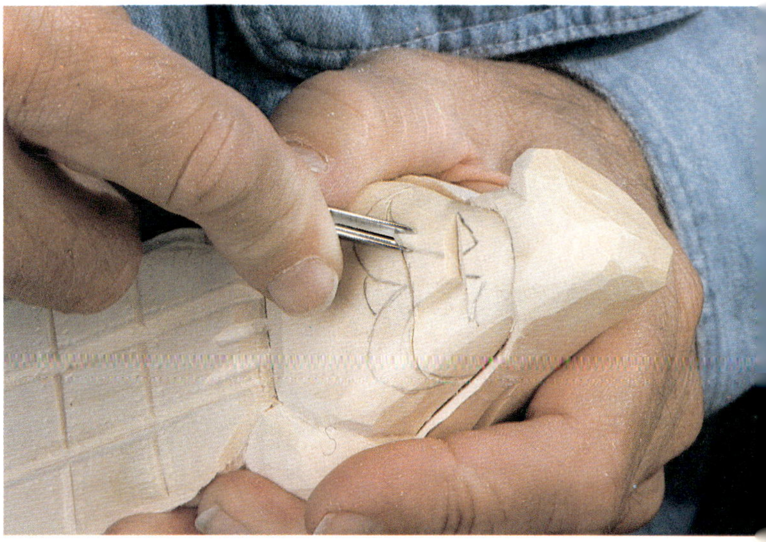

Use the small gouge along either side of the nose to smooth it. The gouge is useful on this larger nose.

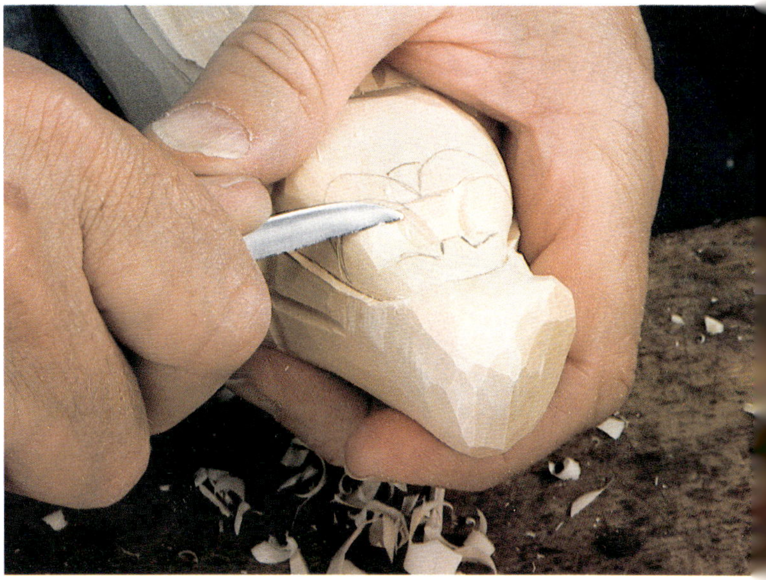

Take your knife and smooth the outside edge of the groove the gouge made.

Round the cheek into the mustache and beard.

I've decided I want the nose to go deeper so I'm going back with the gouge along the sides of the nose.

Cut off the small corners of the nose for nostrils.

Now I'm going to cut the brow back a little so it doesn't overhang so far.

Cut a small piece off the top of the mustache under the nose.

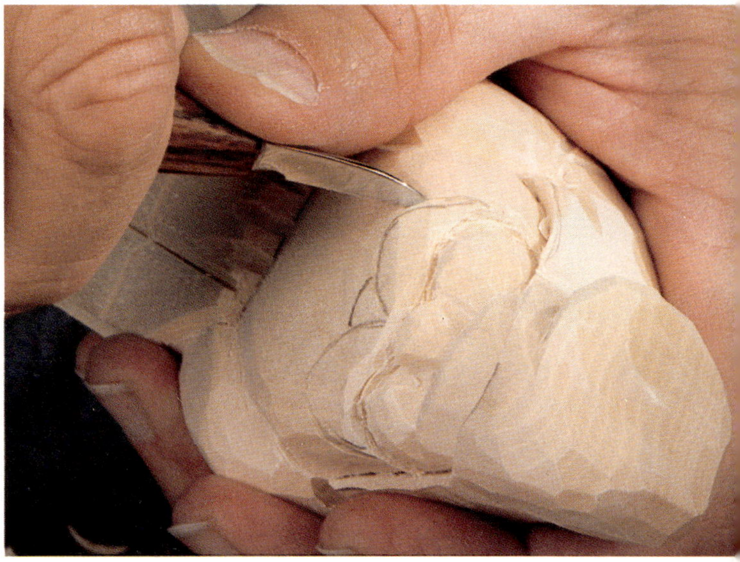

Undercut the mustache.

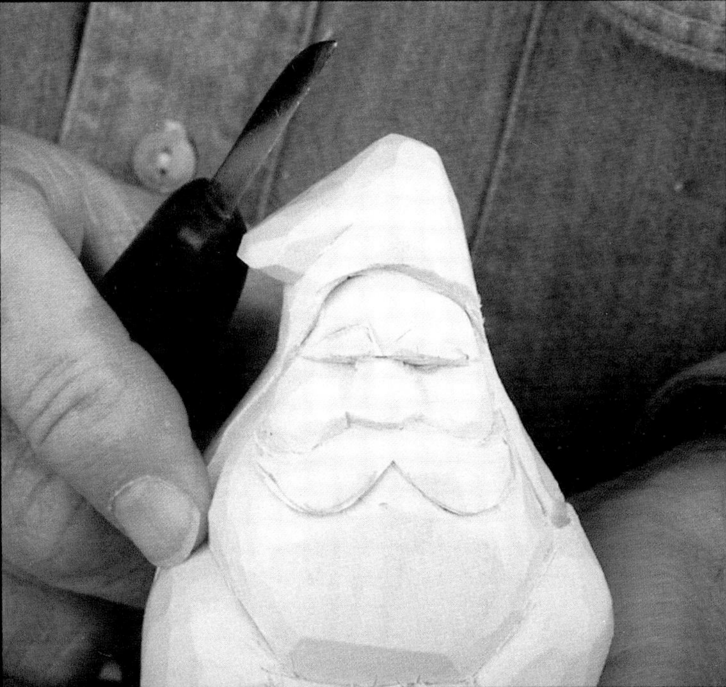

Draw in the eyebrows on the new and improved brow and carve them in.

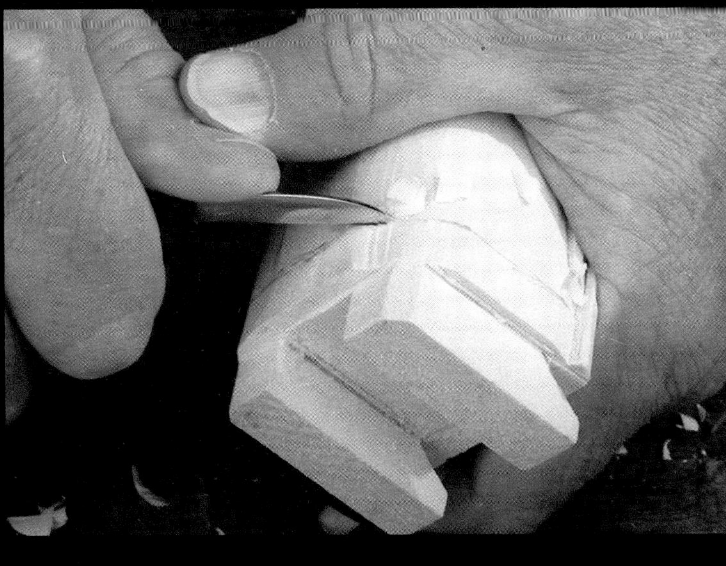

Incise and undercut the fur around the bottom of the robe.

The rounded and finished shoes.

The finished quilt-holding Santa.

Painting

I have been using Ceramcoat from Delta Coatings for as long as I have been painting my carvings. I've found the quality and color to be consistent. The Tompte Red I use on my Santas also matches the blood I sometimes leave on unpainted pieces. If you're happy with your colors, continue to use them.

Painting the quilt holding Santa

The colors I'm using are Tompte Red, Santa's Flesh, White, Black, and Navy Blue mixed with white for some of the quilt patches.

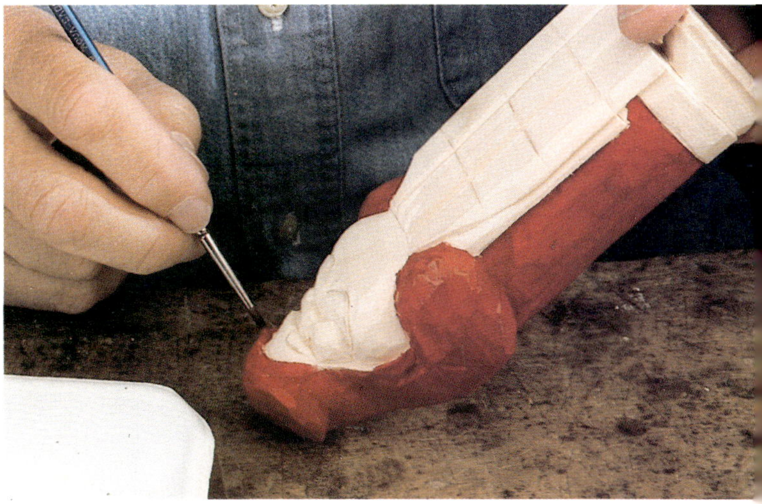

We're going to start with the Tompte Red for the robe. This is the largest area we have to cover. Use a small #3 brush for tight places. Touching up the robe.

Paint the beard and the eyebrows white. We are going to see if the antiquing process will make a shadow that looks like eyes. If not, we'll come back and show you another step.

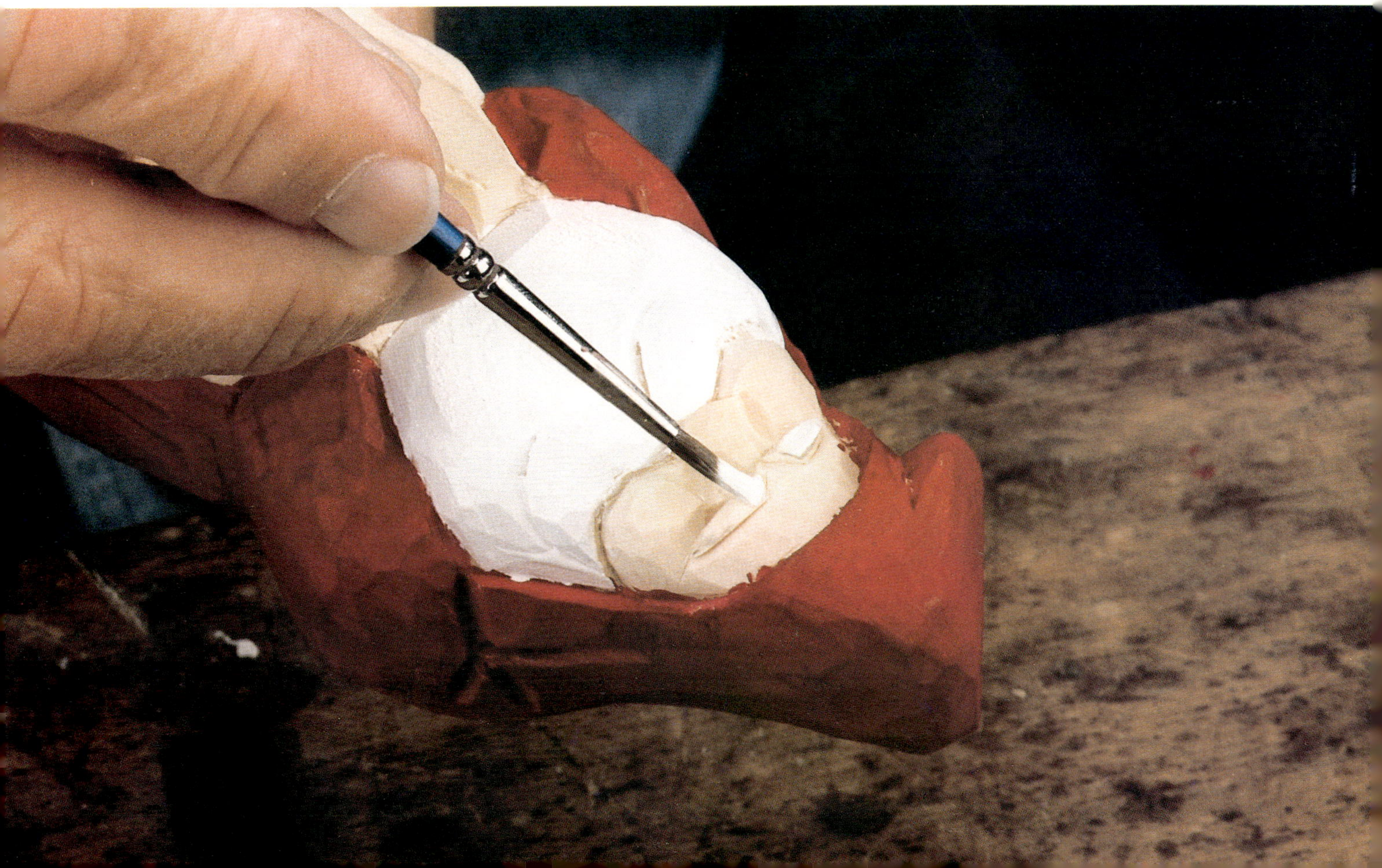

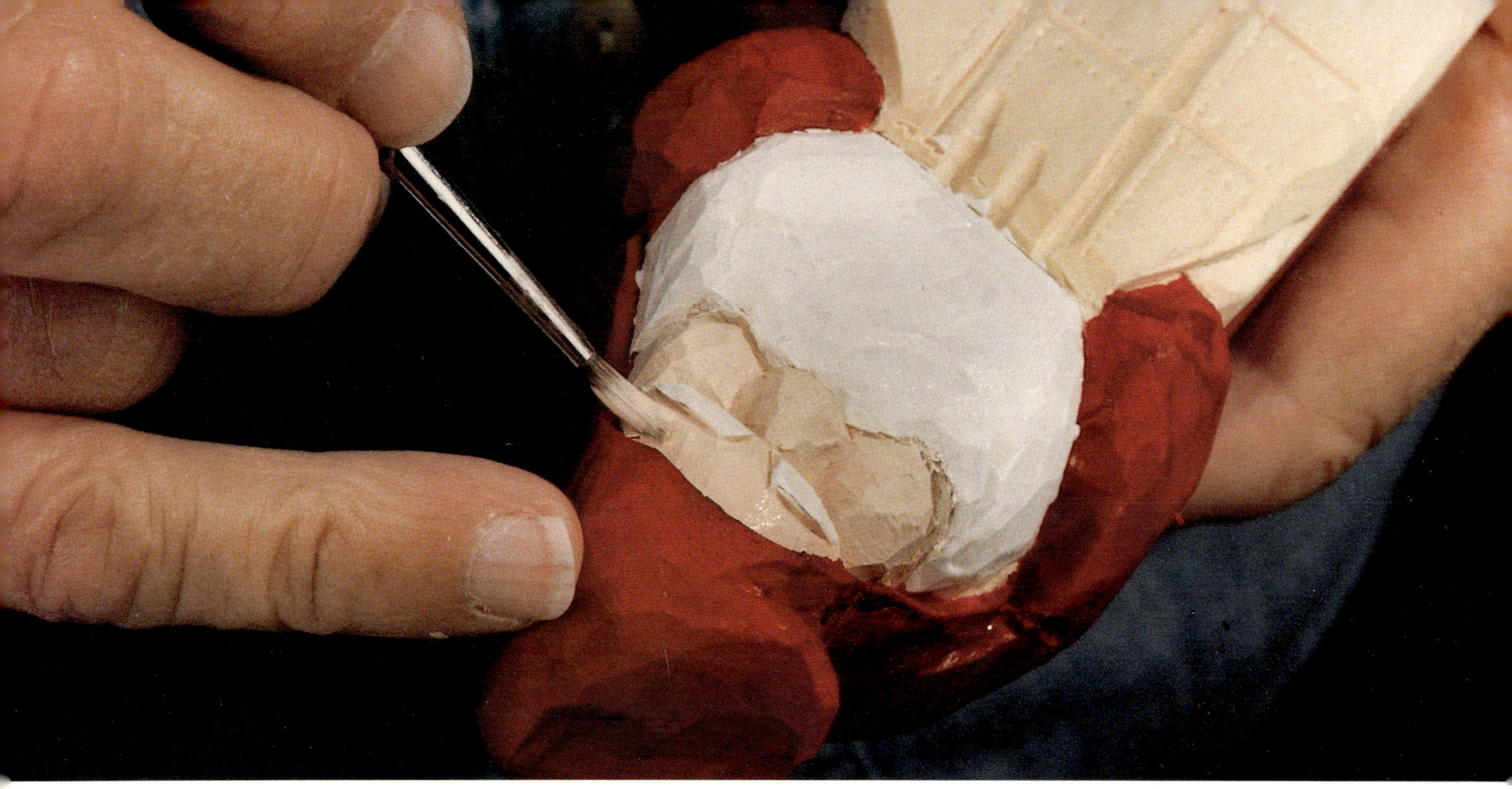

Use Santa's Flesh to cover the face. Be careful to completely cover the face. This is difficult because the flesh color and the natural color of the basswood are so similar. However, if you miss an area it will show up as a dark spot when you antique the figure.

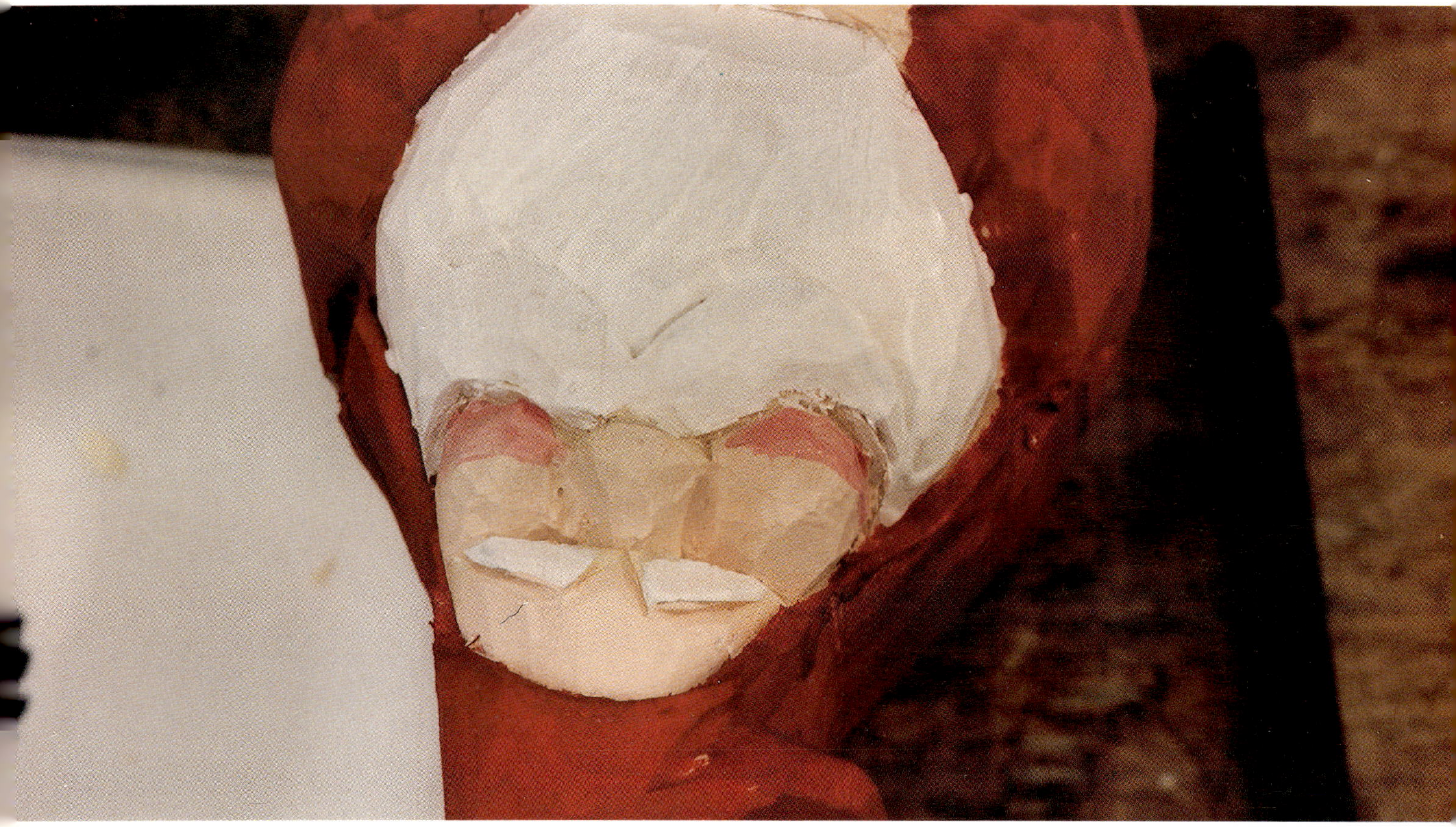

Mix some cheek blush using red and flesh. Don't paint this on in little circles or your Santa will look like a clown.

Use white for the fur trim on the robe. Paint the boots black.

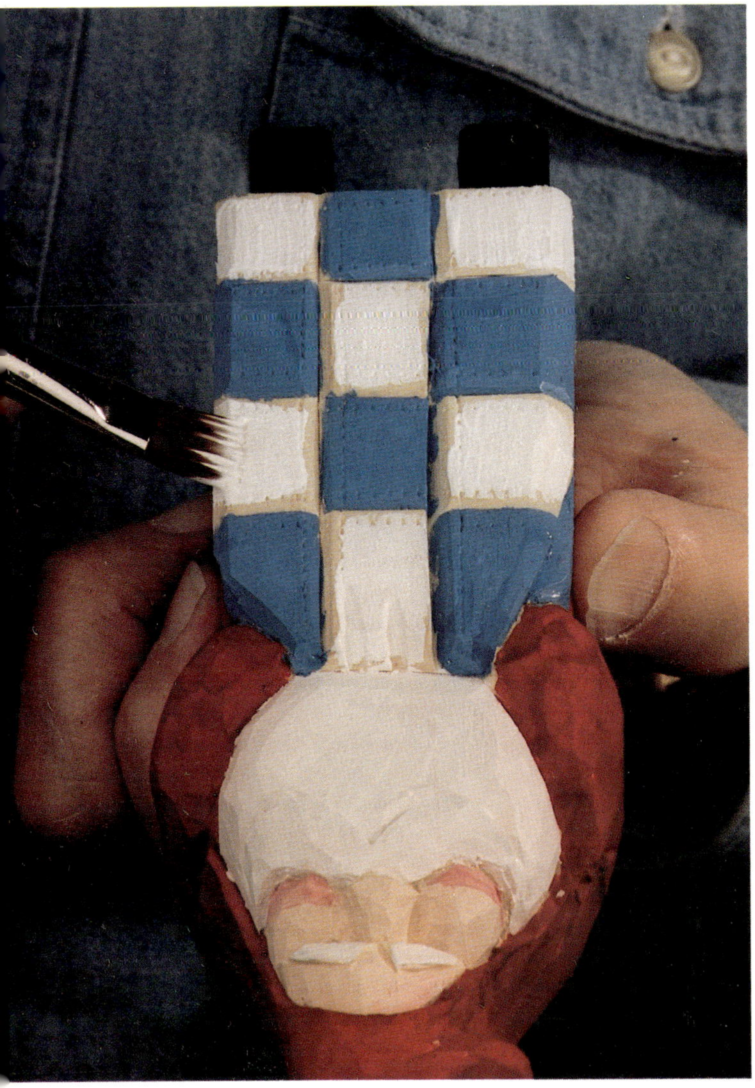

I didn't like the looks of the Navy Blue out of the tube for the quilt so I mixed Navy Blue and White to get a color I was satisfied with. If you do this, make sure you mix enough to cover the entire area the first time. You won't mix the same color twice. Paint alternating squares and the back of the quilt with this blue mix.

Paint the remaining squares white. At this point use Krylon Clear Acrylic Spray #1301 aerosol to coat the Santa and protect the paint.

Once your acrylic paints have dried, it is extremely important to spray your carving with Krylon Clear Coat #1301 aerosol before you give the figure an antique look. Griffin has gone out of business and their polish, long a favorite of mine for "antiquing," has become very hard to find. Now I am using Briwax. They have been in business since 1860 and I feel sure they will be in business for a long time to come. I'm brushing on their Antique Mahogany to coat the entire figure.

Next, take an old tee shirt or diaper and rub the carving with neutral shoe polish. Kiwi works fine. This takes off enough of the Briwax to give the finish that antique look. I like my pieces dark, not garish. If you like, after the polish has dried you may buff it with a shoe brush. Notice how the antiquing has created appropriate shadows for the eyes on this Santa for us.

The finished quilt holding Santa.

The Gallery

Soccer Player Santa

The same colors are used here as were used on the large quilt Santa. The antiquing method is the same for all the Santas.

Baseball Santa

The same colors are used here. In addition, my Atlanta Brave has a blue bill on his baseball cap; his glove and bat are brown.

Boxer Santa

Christmas Green dressing robe, purple trunks, brown boxing gloves, Kim Gold waist band and sash. The bruised eye is purple.

Santa holding Tree

Same as the other Santas. The tree is Christmas Green — what else?